Composing
Qualitative
Research

To my husband Mark,
and my parents Jim and Eleanor, with love.

To my guys Robert, Ian, and Devin, with love.

Composing Qualitative Research

Karen Golden-Biddle
Karen D. Locke

SAGE Publications
International Educational and Professional Publisher
Thousand Oaks   London   New Delhi

For information:

SAGE Publications, Inc.
2455 Teller Road
Thousand Oaks, California 91320
E-mail: order@sagepub.com

SAGE Publications Ltd.
6 Bonhill Street
London EC2A 4PU
United Kingdom

SAGE Publications India Pvt. Ltd.
M-32 Market
Greater Kailash I
New Delhi 110 048 India

Printed in the United States of America

Library of Congress Cataloging-in-Publication Data

Golden-Biddle, Karen.
    Composing qualitative research/authors, Karen Golden-Biddle, Karen D. Locke.
        p. cm.
    Includes bibliographical references and index.
    ISBN 0-8039-7430-2 (cloth).—ISBN 0-8039-7431-0 (pbk.)
    1. Technical writing. I. Locke, Karen D. II. Title.
    T11.G63   1997
    808′.066001—dc21   97-4610

This book is printed on acid-free paper

97 98 99 00 01 02 03 10 9 8 7 6 5 4 3 2 1

Acquiring Editor:	Marquita Flemming
Editorial Assistant:	Frances Borghi
Production Editor:	Sherrise M. Purdum
Production Assistant:	Denise Santoyo
Typesetter/Designer:	Marion Warren
Indexer:	Juniee Oneida
Cover Designer:	Lesa Valdez
Print Buyer	Anna Chin

Contents

Acknowledgments

This book has benefited from many conversations with colleagues about the process and writing of qualitative research. We would like here to specifically acknowledge the work of four colleagues who acted as official reviewers: Jane Dutton, Gary Alan Fine, Barry Goldman, and Bob Sutton. Their thorough reading of the early manuscript and insightful comments both encouraged our work and challenged us to increase its sophistication, clarity, and practical value. We benefited especially by their suggestions to strengthen the metaphor of story, convey the practicality of our points, extend our analyses of what constitutes a "good" story, and to retain our informal tone.

Introduction

We, like many other researchers we know who use qualitative data, have grappled with how to transform our fieldwork experience and vast amounts of data into journal articles. Questions such as the following emerge. What do I want to write about? On which aspects of the data do I focus? How do I construct a compelling argument? How do I reduce what I have to say so that it fits into a journal-sized article? What did I find most interesting and how does it link with theory? How do I depict the actual complexity of life that occurred in the organization? For us, the difficult questions have centered on the following. How do we see the most interesting questions arising from our research? How do we choose the best theoretical location for our work? How do we convey the meaning of our work—its significance and import—so that it resonates with readers?

Through numerous conversations with people about their research and participation in qualitative research panels at academic meetings, we have learned that many of us are asking similar questions on how we write up field-based experiences. Many of these questions concern writing for management journals. Furthermore, based on these conversations and reactions to our earlier work on writing up convincing ethnographic accounts (Golden-Biddle & Locke, 1993), we have become aware of the neglect of these "writing" matters in our doctoral programs. In most cases, we neither teach writing nor talk about it much. This is ironic given that it is a practice that consumes so much of our professional efforts.

This silence on writing, however, occurs at the cost of individual and collective wisdom. The longer we remain silent, the more we mystify the process of writing and transmit that mysticism to future generations of scholars. For example, rather than sharing our experiences about the writing process, through our silence we leave students to their own devices to learn how to write. However, as Becker (1986) has shown, fear, not curious exploration, dominates most graduate students' (and, we add, professors') attempts to learn about writing and to write. Recently, we were able to directly observe this concern among graduate students. We had been invited to conduct a workshop on writing at a large university for an interdisciplinary group of doctoral students who were using a variety of research methods. As the students entered the room, they sat at the back tables and rows of chairs rather than at tables closer to the front. When we asked them to join the closer tables, one of the faculty members told the students not to worry, as they would not be called on to write in public. The students broke out in laughter in response to this comment and began to move to the closer tables.

We write this book, then, to break the silence about writing in graduate schools in organizational studies and, more broadly, to demystify the process of writing. We believe it is important to increase our knowledge about writing; one way in which to begin is by sharing experiences of writing so that we may learn from each other. Ultimately, we believe that if we demystify writing, then we will enhance our own and our intellectual communities' abilities to contribute knowledge about organizing and managing that is more insightful and thoughtful.

Given the book's focus on writing, we have imagined you, the readers, as similar to the people with whom we have conversed about these questions over the years—graduate students who are learning about qualitative research and writing issues for the first time as well as more seasoned qualitative researchers who are exploring ways in which to become more reflective about what they are doing. We expect that those of you who will find this book most interesting and useful will be right in the throes of writing up fieldwork or proposals for research projects or those of you reflecting more generally on the writing process.

Writing About Writing

Recently in sociology and organizational studies, a few authors have begun to write about writing. A book by the sociologist Becker (1986) concretely examines the writing process, including the underlying fears about writing and social organization conventions that hinder clarity in writing. Conceptualizing writing as a form of thinking, he encourages researchers to write early and to write multiple drafts of fieldwork to clarify their thinking. Another sociologist, Fine (1988), develops 10 practical "commandments" about writing. In particular, he emphasizes that because all writing is socially situated, social scientists should have particular audiences and purposes in mind as they write. He also encourages researchers to use literary techniques such as metaphors and poetic language to bring arguments to life for readers. Richardson (1994) also takes up the matter of writing by suggesting it is a method of knowing, a way of finding out about ourselves and our topics. In her article, she examines traditional and experimental formats for writing and provides some interesting suggestions for adopting the view of writing as a method of knowing.

The work by Gephart (1986, 1988) is most likely the first such work by a member of the management field to address writing matters. In this work, he examines rhetorical conventions, such as the use of passive or quasi-passive voice and the creation of gaps, to support and legitimate arguments based on quantitative data. Furthermore, he has used ironic analysis to illuminate how such texts construct the appearance of objectivity in conveying truth, in large part through its rhetorical practices. The work by Van Maanen (1988, 1995) also has paved the way to examine writing in organizational studies. In his *Tales of the Field,* Van Maanen (1988) identifies three forms of ethnographic writing (realist, confessional, and impressionistic) and the writing conventions associated with each, including how the author is depicted in the text and how reality is represented. In his more recent edited volume, *Representation in Ethnography,* Van Maanen (1995) incorporates rhetoric by bringing to center stage both the construction and convincingness of textual arguments as well as the readers' reading of those arguments. Finally, Wolcott (1990) develops some hands-on and very useful suggestions for moving along the writing process in its various phases, as reflected by his chapter titles: "Getting Going," "Keeping Going," "Tightening Up," "Finishing Up," and "Getting Published."

In writing this book, we owe an intellectual debt to these works. How nice to have an emerging tradition of writing about writing to draw on! We also have been informed by and draw on the work of rhetoric and literary theory in the social sciences. In particular, we have been influenced by the works of Booth (1961, 1967) and Iser (1978, 1989), who have incorporated into literary criticism the notions of implied author and reader and active texts and readers, and by the works of Knorr-Cetina (1981), Latour (1987), Latour and Woolgar (1986), McCloskey (1985, 1990, 1994), and Selzer (1993), who have examined directly the rhetorical dimension of scientific texts.

Our book also differs from these works in that we seek to provide a systematic yet very concrete approach to the writing up of qualitative research. Although we definitely bring a literary and rhetorical understanding to this book, we seek to translate this knowledge and perspective into specific and critical issues that we, as writers, face in constructing written accounts of our fieldwork. In so doing, our major focus concerns how to make contextually developed theoretical points to an audience. Our book also differs from previous work by our exclusive attention to publishing in management journals. Thus we do not ask the question of whether we should publish in books or journals; we assume that researchers will choose the medium for them. Because most of the questions we have received—and, frankly, most of our own questions—have focused on writing up fieldwork for journals, we concern ourselves exclusively with that outlet.

Writing Our Fieldwork

In the 7 or so years that we have been thinking, reading, and writing about writing, we have come to believe that transforming qualitative research efforts into written textual form concerns much more than the rational presentation of data; we do not simply gather "facts" in the field that speak for themselves and make our contribution apparent to all readers. We certainly have never faced a situation as clear as that, although often we wish we had! Nor do we know of anyone else who has faced such a clear situation (cf. Becker, 1986; Feldman, 1995). Indeed, if this were the case, then the often-heard injunction to "just write up" (Van Maanen, 1988) our interviews and other field notes would be easily implemented.

Instead, we have come to believe that the major task of writing up our research involves figuring out how to make contextually grounded, theoretical points that are viewed as a contribution by the relevant professional community of readers. As writers who have literally gone into organizations to collect data, our writing task involves developing theoretical points, contextualizing those points in field data, and convincing our readers of the uniqueness of these grounded theoretical points. We do not simply present facts that stand alone; rather, we craft arguments intended to persuade readers that we have something new to offer relative to extant theoretical conversation. At the personal level, the crafting and shaping of manuscripts involve ourselves as authors, the organizational setting and members with whom we interacted for longer or shorter periods of time, and the arguments we make and how we develop them in the text. At a more general but still influential level, our writing task takes into consideration the academic institutional setting, with its associated norms for "doing science" and journal review processes, and our largely academic community of readers.

Focus on "Story"

So, how do we craft manuscripts that make unique theoretical points that are contextually grounded? In this book, we call on the metaphor of "story" to illuminate matters of writing for management journals as we attempt to answer this question. By invoking this metaphor, we are better able to explore writing matters such as crafting storylines, shaping the storyteller in the text, and negotiating the retelling of our stories in interaction with journal reviewers and editors. The distinguishing characteristic of stories is that they possess a discernible framework for structuring the written account. Specifically, stories are grounded in events and provide a narrative structure that organizes those events into beginnings, middles, and ends. Furthermore, they provide explanations of the turns in events through the development of plots.

One day, while we were writing this book, Karen Locke's young son, Ian, showed her a picture that he had drawn in school that day. The picture portrayed a snowman and had three separate scenes, representing the beginning, middle, and ending of the story that Ian had crafted. The first scene showed a snowman with a top hat and smile. The second scene introduced the sun along with the snowman as he had looked in the first scene. In the final scene, the sun was still shining, but all that remained of the snowman was a puddle and the top hat. Very simply, yet elegantly, Ian's story of the snowman both showed the chronological progression of events over time and incorporated a plot, or storyline: The introduction of the sun had caused the snowman to melt.

Similarly, as qualitative researchers, we observe organizational events and members' interpretations of those events as they unfold over time. Indeed, what we offer in the way of distinctive knowledge is a process-based view of events in organizations; we examine the "how" as well as the meaning of organizational phenomena. The difference between our stories and Ian's story of the snowman is that we then use this local knowledge as grounding for the development of our theoretical points—our plots. We seek to develop theoretical points that are based on existing academic conversations in the literature and add something new to those conversations. Thus we link organizational members' actions and interpretations of what happened with the theoretical conversation to construct unique points or novel arguments about what might have happened. In the case of the snowman, for example, we might momentarily imagine the snowman as organization and link Ian's plot to some theoretical discourse. So, we could argue that organizations are strategically vulnerable to certain aspects of the environment or that a liability of newness exists for young organizations. In this book, then, we view the common genus as story construction and storytelling, and we view both the members' interpretations and our theoretical points as being a specific form of the common genus.

The issue in writing up qualitative research, then, becomes not whether we tell stories but rather how conscious we are of the stories that we tell. Do we know both what constitutes our theoretical points and how we develop them throughout the manuscript? Have we considered which members' voices we use in retelling organizationally based stories? How aware are we of both *what* we write about and *how* we write? Writing up qualitative research involves both the "what" and the "how" as interdependent components of the written product (as does all research). Yet it is the "how" of our writing that usually is overlooked.

By invoking the metaphor of stories, we notice the "how" more readily and are better able to integrate it with the "what" of our writing. For example, we notice (a) a beginning, or how an extant theoretical conversation looks before the proposed study, including associated problems or omissions in that conversation; (b) an ending, or how the present study changes that conversation by resolving the identified problems; and (c) a middle, showing evidence to support the proposed change in theoretical conversation. Similarly, Weick (1995) suggests, "In a full defense of an idea, the author shows how some display looks different before and after it is viewed using the innovation that is proposed" (p. 294).

Additionally, by invoking the story metaphor, we notice more readily other aspects of the manuscript. For example, what types of characters do the storytellers establish in the text, and how do the characters persuade readers to regard the theoretical points as unique and important? Furthermore, do the storytellers assume an objective impartial stance, implying that they are reporting the "truth"? Or, do they insert themselves into the text more explicitly through the use of personal pronouns? Finally, how do authors use data to bring their theoretical points to life?

Organization of Chapters

We have organized this book according to the various facets of the story construction and telling processes. Chapter 1, "The Style and Practice of Our Professional Writing," explores taken-for-granted assumptions in our profession that influence, and more particularly mystify, the process of writing up qualitative research. As such, this chapter provides critical background information for the specific discussions in Chapters 2-5. Chapter 2, "Crafting Storylines," examines the story metaphor in greater depth, focusing on how authors craft storylines, or theoretical points, that are offered as unique contributions to the literature. It highlights the complication-resolution composition of storylines in which authors build on and problematize the extant literature and offer resolutions to the identified problems. Chapter 3, "Developing the Storyline," examines how authors contextualize theoretical points in their field experience. Specifically, we show how, in developing their storylines, authors use field data for two purposes: to take readers "there" (e.g., to convey the vitality of everyday life in the field) and to bridge the worlds of the field and the reader by signifying the theoretical meanings of the data. Chapter 4, "Characterizing the Storyteller," shows how authors construct the storyteller in journal articles. Here we examine how authors develop the character of institutional scientist in their texts and also differentiate themselves as individual scientists. Chapter 5, "Rewriting the Story," examines the construction and reconstruction of our stories within the larger institutional context of the academy and, in particular, during the peer review process. Here we profile the review processes associated with seven published articles and incorporate actual reviewer and editor comments as well as author responses. Finally, in our "Concluding Comments," we share some closing thoughts on writing matters.

In each chapter, we use actual examples from our own and others' published writings drawn from three of the mainstream U.S. journals in organization studies: *Academy of Management Journal, Administrative Science Quarterly,* and *Or-*

ganization Science. To distinguish these examples from other referenced works, we list them separately in an appendix. In addition, in keeping with the informal style of writing we use in this book, we reference the authors of these works by using both their last and their (usually more informal) first names on their first mentions in each chapter.

Each of these examples uses wholly qualitative data in its presentation. No particular criteria were applied to the selection of the articles discussed except that they illustrate especially well the aspect of writing under discussion. The examples are by no means exhaustive. Indeed, there are many other articles in established journals outside of the United States such as *Organization Studies, Journal of Management Studies,* and *Human Relations.* Furthermore, there are articles in journals that have been created explicitly to be "nontraditional" such as the *Journal of Management Inquiry* or *Organization.* As you read, we would hope that both your knowledge and repertoire of others' qualitative work, as well as your own work, will provide additional illustrations.

A final note. Throughout our writing of this book, we have been well aware of two primary and sometimes conflicting motivations. On the one hand, we especially want to provide first-time researchers with support to make the transition from the field to writing a creative, rather than a debilitating, one. To this end, throughout the book we identify and illustrate a number of rhetorical practices that authors use to craft and bring home their theoretical points. On the other hand, however, we want to avoid espousing a normative "how to" guide for writing up field data. We are not advocating one right or correct way to write up data. To do so would dampen the creativity in each person's writing adventures and most likely would result in uninteresting and increasingly similar work. We certainly do not want to create a "boilerplate" approach to the writing up of qualitative research. So, in this book we have sought very intentionally to examine what a wide variety of authors using qualitative data in journals are up to in their work. The outcome, we hope, is that as conscious writers and readers of the stories we tell in organizational studies, we all will contribute to the construction of knowledge that is more innovative, thoughtful, reasoned, and insightful.

1

The Style and Practice of Our Professional Writing

*W*riting this book underscores that whatever else we may be as researchers and scholars, we are at the core a profession of text writers. The knowledge our discipline has assembled about organizations is composed and maintained in written texts. As professional organization scholars, our research efforts are known, in large part, through our written products. The papers and monographs we write stand symbolically for the data gathering and analytic efforts we put into our organizational scholarship. Additionally, as we are all too aware, our ability to be members in good standing in the profession revolves around the ability to write our discipline's professional texts; our careers, visibility, and professional mobility all are implicated in our writing (Frost & Taylor, 1995).

Indeed, as is true of other knowledge-creating professions (Bazerman & Paradis, 1991), organizational studies constitutes itself and maintains much of its organization, power, and work through its network of texts such as journals, books, and newsletters. For example, these texts frame and select the topics and issues to which our discipline pays attention. Additionally, those individuals who are in positions to decide on the disposition of these texts, such as editors and members of editorial boards, are widely viewed as enjoying considerable professional power. Moreover, embedded in these texts are taken-for-granted assumptions, our field's normative traditions, concerning what we write up and how we do so. Like it or not—and sometimes we do and sometimes we don't—in this profession we are about writing, and this writing sets the terms of much of our work lives.

This chapter examines what we understand by the term "writing" in the context of our professional activities. Our discussion of the writing in our discipline's texts simultaneously examines it from two overlapping and related perspectives: the style of the writing we produce for and find in journal articles and the nature of writing as a practice in the process of creating knowledge.

The Style of Professional Writing: Unadorned and Disembodied

What is a research article? What kind of writing, if any, distinguishes it? The more typical answer is that it is a straightforward account of researchers' investigations of some aspect of organizational life. As such a report, we understand that this form of professional writing should provide an impersonal and detached demonstration of the results of our investigative procedures as well as an explanation of the work's significance to existing knowledge about a domain of theoretical interest to organizational scholars.

Following writing conventions in the "sciences," the writing in these reports generally is taken to be minimally expressive so that discovered phenomena can be reflected as clearly as possible in the text. This is a "windowpane" model of language (Brooks & Warren, 1938) in which scientists carefully avoid in their scientific prose "all associations, emotional coloring, and implications of attitude and judgment" (p. 4). Such nonornamental prose is well suited to an understanding of the journal article's function as transferring information gleaned from the field to the library, that academically removed knowledge repository. This Kantian perspective on writing, as Rorty (1982) points out, construes writing as an "unfortunate necessity" (p. 94), a sort of reluctant intermediary between an investigated field and disciplinary knowledge. Similar views have been articulated in organizational studies by a number of scholars. For example, Pinder and Bourgeois (1982) urge researchers to "deliberately strive" to avoid all literary tropes in their writing so as to "tie scientific communication to observable phenomena by way of direct reference and ostentation" (p. 646). These authors urge us to tell the simple truth, plain and unvarnished, about the aspects of organizational life we observe.

However, we find the style of scientific writing to be neither plain nor simple. It is a way of writing that we have had to learn. In fact, we suspect that very few of us start out by writing the "academicspeak" of our profession. Rather, the language and writing practices that symbolize the culture of science traditionally are transmitted across generations of academics. As members of the profession, we have to pick up that special anonymous disciplinary code in which "it is concluded that" and only "the data," not researchers, "suggest" anything. During graduate studies, Karen Locke can remember submitting a course paper in which she was present in the first person—"I, therefore, conclude . . ."—only to be told that it was unacceptable. Being present in the text in that way was a violation of the professional code that required her to write in the disembodied voice of scientific demonstration. She had to learn to write herself out of her texts and let "the findings speak for themselves." In so doing, she symbolically adhered to and transmitted the view of writing as straightforward reporting of observed phenomena.

Furthermore, if the writing of scientific style does not come naturally, then neither does the reading of it. For readers outside these disciplinary boundaries, as we are all too well aware, many of the practices associated with the scientific style obfuscate our points. Ironically, the straightforward reporting is anything but straightforward. For example, extensive use of the passive voice to keep the writer/researcher out of the text (Gephart, 1986), makes the writing cumbersome and obtuse. This inaccessibility of our writing is particularly troublesome in an applied discipline such as organizational studies where we essentially have two audiences for our work. Presumably, we would like not only academics but also practicing managers to read and comment on our work. Paradoxically, in conforming to our implicit assumptions regarding a scientific style of writing, our writing may well discourage a managerial audience from engaging it.

The Practice of Professional Writing: "Just Write It Up" . . . There Is a Lot More to It

The assumptions of objectivity and straightforward reporting that are embedded in the style of our professional writing carry over to the practice of writing. That is, these assumptions suggest that the writing task involves simply and straightforwardly documenting what we have observed. However, this "it's as plain as the nose on your face" assumption does not square with the experience of actively writing up research findings. Our disciplinary writing is a much more complicated, social, and human performance than the preceding narrow positivist conception allows (Hunter, 1990). When we sit in front of our terminals with our piles of field notes, transcripts, and analytic memos, expecting to "just write it up" as Van Maanen (1988) indicates he was told to do, we discover all too clearly that it is not that simple.

Write It Up!

Let us look closer at this injunction, which conceives of writing as an easy "isn't it obvious?" process. It suggests an uncomplicated transition between the analytically condensed "who said or did what to whom and with what effects" recorded in the field notes and the finished journal article. However, the apparent effortlessness intimated by the injunction masks a number of key and laborious tasks that the writing up of qualitative data surfaces and requires.

Write It Up,
But Write What Up?

First, this injunction implies that the meaning relevant to organization studies, and around which the manuscript will be oriented, lies already formed and waiting to be picked up. The "it" to be written up obviously is not the stream of recorded conversations and actions or the carefully produced analytic tables but rather the significance of these details of organization life for broader phenomena and processes. Contrary to the windowpane assumptions of findings as self-evident, we never yet have had a piece of data tell us its significance!

For us, the injunction of write it up belies the artful and often arduous process of writing the field data for what it all means. As we work with the field notes, transcripts, and analytic memoranda through which we document and pattern our experience in the field, what we are doing is thinking about that experience to make some sense out of it. In our sense-making efforts, we think about the field experience in relation to other comparable situations and in relation to what other researchers and scholars have said about similar situations. Conversely, we also think about other researchers' theories in light of our particular experience. We do not write up all that we saw or heard or were told. Rather, we write up what all of our thinking and comparing has led us to believe our field experience means (Watson, 1995).

Furthermore, even after we discern meaning in our fieldwork, we still encounter difficulties. This is especially the case when we write up our data for journal articles. Typically, our data surface many issues that we find important and worthy of telling. However, because a journal article imposes very real spatial constraints on our writing, we cannot tell all the meanings we discerned; we must make choices. In a real sense, we have to set aside aspects of our investigative experience that, although important to us and even integral to our experiences of field life, do not help us to develop the particular meanings and insights we have chosen to write about. The trade-off between conveying some or all of the meaning discerned in the field experience stands in starkest relief when we write for journals with space limitations, although it also is present to a lesser degree in writing books.

For Karen Golden-Biddle, this trade-off is most vivid. Although she has published one journal article from her dissertation fieldwork (Golden, 1992), she has not yet been able to figure out how to tell in journal article form what, to her, is the central story of her fieldwork: that in a large

Fortune 500 organization, managers appreciate the practices and beliefs developed by past generations of managers and actively transmit and seek to enact them in the present. Early drafts telling this story have met with colleague skepticism. How, they question, can a *Fortune* 500 organization survive in today's changing environment when it is oriented to the past? For her, the difficulty in telling this story centers on the lack of space in journal articles to sufficiently detail what constitutes the traditional cornerstone of this organization and on discerning the most insightful theoretical positioning.

To the extent that we choose to develop and write about particular meanings disclosed in our fieldwork, we can regard the "it" that we write about as constructed. Few among us today would accept the proposition that researchers go into the field and gather up the pieces of reality laying around waiting to be gleaned. We appreciate instead that researchers, as well as organization members, shape the experienced reality. In much the same way, we reject the notion of writing as a transmission of an objective reality. We agree with the literary critics Booth (1961) and Iser (1978, 1989) and with the sociologist Gusfield (1981) that the hand of the writer and the eyes of the reader shape all written works, even those in science. Our written products are crafted works.

Write It Up, But for Whom?

The injunction also conceals the readers for whom we write: the particular disciplinary community comprising the audience for the journal article. As such, our audience is a sort of concealed participant in the writing process. There is no getting around it; all manuscripts are addressed to a particular audience (Booth, 1961; Burke, 1950; Iser, 1978). When we choose to direct our work toward mainstream academic journals, we privilege an academic audience over a managerial one. In turn, our selected audience exerts its influence over our writing. Our professional community sets the topical boundaries for our writing, broadly delimiting the phenomena that fall within the domain of organizational studies. Our audience also broadly sets out the manuscripts' structure and progression: the movement from literature review to methods, results, and a concluding discussion. Those disciplinary writing conventions allow readers to consider our work as coming from one who is a member of the scientific community. To shun the use of such established forms and formats is to bait denial of a forum for our work within the profession (Lyne, 1993).

So, we write up the research findings for a general audience of organization theorists who, as we have indicated, have their own compositional conventions and, of course, insider language. But, more specifically, we write for an audience of researchers and scholars also interested in the particular organizational processes and phenomena addressed by the putative work. Organizational studies, like any other disciplinary community, is composed of small overlapping social systems delineated by interest in a particular phenomenon or idea— " 'specialties,' 'problem domains,' 'research areas' or 'research networks' " (Knorr-Cetina, 1981, p. 9). Typically, our work is directed toward one or perhaps two of these specialty audiences.

Again, a personal example. Karen Locke still can remember quite vividly sitting with pages and pages of carefully worked out analyses, documenting and explaining the patterning of comedic episodes in a tertiary care hospital (Locke, 1996a). Certainly, she had a tale to tell about doctors, patient anxiety, and comedy. However, the topic of organizational humor is one that, at best, has received only scattered and erratic attention. She had a tale for which only a small—some would say marginal—audience existed, as the very modest literature on organizational humor attests. However, when the doctors were recast as service providers and the patients as coproviders in the service delivery process, she demarcated a much broader audience for the work by embedding a research account about one aspect of life in a hospital in a broader discussion of emotionality in client-provider relationships. Writing it up, then, necessarily incorporates the understanding that the meanings we choose to develop and articulate in our work must be directed toward and lay claim to a specific, and preferably mainstream, audience within the organizational studies community.

Furthermore, although an audience finds engaging the details of work life in particular organizations that qualitative research yields—whether those details describe a tertiary care hospital (Locke, 1996a), a funeral home (Barley, 1983), a bill collection agency (Sutton, 1991), a health maintenance organization (Prasad, 1993), and so on—our disciplinary audiences are primarily motivated by interest in theory. Such audiences, constituted along particular theoretical lines, are interested in these details, but only as illustrations of theory or point of view (Langer, 1964). Our disciplinary manuscripts are addressed toward particular theoretical lines that interest ourselves and our readers. For example, in the vignette just described, research on comedy in physician-client relationships ultimately was directed at two theoretical audiences: one interested in the area of organizational emotion and the other in the area of service relationships.

McClosky (1990) uses the metaphor of a conversation to describe the theoretical interests and literature-building activities of our disciplinary audience. As a community, we have audiences interested in, and ongoing conversations about, organizational emotions, about service relationships, about organizational culture, about the relationship between technology and structure, about processes of executive succession, and so on. In keeping with the metaphor, when we direct our work toward a particular theoretical audience, we are looking to join in, not just eavesdrop on (Becker, 1986), their conversation. Thus, when we write up our work, we use the discussion of existing literature to locate the study in a particular conversation; but more than that, we translate our experiences in the field for particular theoretical audiences.

Write It Up, But Under What Terms Will It Be Granted a Disciplinary Audience?

Finally, the injunction to write it up veils the terms under which our work will be given a reading by the community of organizational theorists. We do not join the conversation until our work is published, and our disciplinary community has an admission requirement for inclusion in this "public" theoretical discourse. Certainly, the work must be judged to be in some sense "true," that is, to authentically depict the organizational situation studied (Golden-Biddle & Locke, 1993). But it also must be significant. As researchers, we must somehow show that our work brings something new to the conversation. We must have a story to tell that will make a difference in and change the extant conversation.

Taken together, then, the injunction to write it up conceals how we shape field notes and analytic memoranda in light of existing conversations in organizational studies. It also masks the crafting of our story: how we couple theory and data to develop coherent and insightful points that make a difference in, and contribute to, the discipline's theoretical conversations. Ultimately, the injunction masks the production of research reports as human constructions, intended to persuade a particular community that what they have to say is both "true" and important to the domains we study. In unmasking and unpacking "just write it up," then, we see that individual researchers shape and form the findings, invoke and delimit an audience that will be interested in the work, and seek to convince the audience that their work makes a difference in our understanding of a particular organizational phenomenon. Writing is thus revealed to be a much more active, creative, and human process than the windowpane model would have us believe.

The Style and Practice of Professional Writing: Interested and Persuasive Discourse

As our preceding discussion hints, even when our research articles provide coherent stories that point to particular theoretical contributions, they are not automatically construed as knowledge. They have to be accorded the status of knowledge; for example, they must be seen as true and significant, first by a small group of reviewers who represent our disciplinary community and then by the wider community itself. What counts as knowledge, then, is a matter of disciplinary consensus (Aronson, 1984; Latour, 1987; Latour & Woolgar, 1986; Rorty, 1967). Whether the research will count as knowledge or not depends on whether it is subsequently cited, that is, written into other research reports as part of the literature review summarizing what we know about a given topic. Only when it is cited and its findings are used in future published articles will a piece of research have achieved the status of contributing to knowledge in the field. If it is seriously challenged by its intended readers—or even worse, completely ignored—then its claim to knowledge will have been denied (Gilbert, 1976; Winsor, 1993).

Accordingly, we can view journal articles as proposals directed to particular audiences for them to legitimate our grounded, theoretical points as knowledge (Aronson, 1984; Gilbert, 1976). As proposals of knowledge, they require adjudication and some accrediting action on the part of their disciplinary audience before they are accorded the status of knowledge. When we submit and publish our work, then, we are putting out proposals that constitute a link between us as authors and our audience (Cozzens, 1985). Furthermore, our knowledge proposals are constructed as, and intended to be taken as, authoritative (Spector & Kitsuse, 1977). Our authority to write is disclosed in the presentation of data, in the authors' expositions of the history of knowledge development in the area (as well as delineation of problems in it), in the account of the investigative and analytic operations performed, and so on.

Additionally, we do not simply lay out knowledge proposals for our audience to take or leave. As we already have indicated, our audience's accrediting actions are highly sought after. We write from an interested perspective; we have a personal stake in the outcomes of our work. At the same time as we write to explicate our theoretical points, we write to advance them. We construct our research products with an eye toward audience reaction. In so doing, we write to persuade others of the contribution of our work.

Interestingly, until the late 1970s, most academicians considered scientific texts to be nonpersuasive. Science was viewed as a special discourse operating outside the domain of rhetoric (Selzer, 1993). Whereas artists were thought to persuade through language, scientists were thought to persuade through logic and evidence (Gusfield, 1981). Rhetoric was and, unfortunately, still today is considered something of a dirty word, one that automatically invokes the qualifying adjectives "mere" and "empty." This image of rhetoric, however, rests on an essentially monologic view of texts (Billig, 1993; Mulkay, 1985). It presents authors as omnipotent, delivering their powerful words to a hapless readership that can only deliver up its highly sought accreditation with "tears, cheers, and helpless admiration" (Billig, 1993, p. 122). What a glorious writer's fantasy! Of course, this distorted image of rhetoric overestimates the effect our texts have on our readers at the same time as it underestimates the effect our readers have on our texts.

In recent years, the view that scientific writing is arhetorical is being replaced with an understanding that our writing is indeed rhetorical by virtue of our constructing theoretical arguments intended for an audience (McCloskey, 1994). During the past decade, a number of disciplines have turned a rhetorical lens to their own writing practices. For example, research traditions and new conversations are developing in anthropology (Clifford, 1983; Geertz, 1973, 1988; Marcus, 1980; Marcus & Cushman, 1982; Marcus & Fischer, 1986), economics (McCloskey, 1985, 1994), and sociology (Atkinson, 1990; Edmonson, 1984; Hunter, 1990). More recently, organizational scholars also have begun to analyze their own texts (Calas & Smircich, 1991; Golden-Biddle & Locke, 1993; Kilduff, 1993; Mumby & Putnam, 1992; Van Maanen, 1988, 1995; Watson, 1995). However, although a number of authors have addressed this topic, the work has yet to cohere into a systematic investigative tradition.

The authors just cited have noted that, even when we adhere in our writing to the strictest conventions of science—when we remove all personal associations, use technical terms, rely very heavily on presented data, and so on—our texts are nevertheless persuasive. They persuade our audience that we are competent scientists whose work and findings are credible. For example, when Knorr-Cetina (1981) describes how research chemists fashion a textual linearity out of a nonlinear research process, she provides an example of how these authors persuade by adhering to the conventions of presenting the research process. Similarly, March and Simon's (1958) foundational text, *Organizations,* has been praised for its avoidance of rhetorical devices such as figurative language (Pinder & Bourgeois, 1982). However, as Kilduff's (1993) analysis of this work demonstrates, although the authors clearly stated that they were sacrificing the literary in favor of a scientific style, they nonetheless relied on various textual strategies to configure as severely limited and inadequate prior research and theorizing on organizations. There is no escaping it. As soon as we frame ideas and craft theoretical points for presentation to some audience, we are engaging in rhetoric or persuasive discourse.

Paying attention to the textual construction of our grounded theoretical points does not undermine their truth value. Such attention simply provides us with a more sophisticated perspective from which to read and write them. Our choice does not concern whether to write persuasive discourse. That is given. Instead, it concerns how conscious we will become of our persuasive efforts. By paying attention to both what theoretical points we develop and how we argue them, we begin to demystify our professional writing and become more reflexive about our own and others' writing.

Indeed, for those who read disciplinary texts with an eye on their textual practices, it does not take long to discern literary elements. These range from those that are quite small to others that are more figural in the text. Let us consider some examples that provide a taste of the relationship between the knowledge we generate in our discipline and how we use language to convey that knowledge. As an illustration of more diminutive literary elements, look at the use of a single qualifying word to help the following articles construct consensual theoretical positions within various conversations (Locke & Golden-Biddle, in press).

> There is considerable agreement among those who have studied mentoring that in order to understand fully the nature and impact of this developmental relationship, it is necessary to examine how it changes over time. (Kram, 1983, p. 609)

Theorists largely agree that individual power in organizations is the ability to control others, to exercise discretion, to get one's own way. (Biggart & Hamilton, 1984, p. 540)

Further, as Mintzberg (1973:38) wrote, "Virtually every empirical study of management time allocation draws attention to the great proportion of time spent in verbal communication . . . [and] my own findings bear this out." (quoted in Gronn, 1983, p. 2)

In all of these examples, the authors assert that organizational scholars share similar perspectives about some aspect of organizational life so as to theoretically position their own studies. Accordingly, the use of the qualifiers "considerable," "largely," and "virtually" in these claims permits the authors to highlight that significant agreement does indeed exist among scholars without, of course, asserting that the perspectives are unanimously held.

A larger and more familiar literary device is the metaphor. Following are three examples of its use to help advance the knowledge claims of organization theorists.

In 1988, Connie Gersick published her "punctuated model" of how teams progressed that, she argued, challenged long-standing models of group development based on a hierarchical progression of groups through universal stages. A central theoretical point made in her manuscript, then, concerns the difference between the model of group development represented in the literature and the model that her research suggested. To highlight the distinction between the two models, she draws on the metaphor of a football game to under-score what she found:

> It was like seeing the game of football as progressing through a structure of quarters (phases) with a major half-time break, versus seeing the game as progressing in a characteristic sequence of distinguishable styles of play (stages). (p. 16)

This literary device is used both to portray the essential properties of her proposed model and to clearly distinguish it from the prevailing model. At the same time as the metaphor helps to convey the results of her research inquiries and her theoretical points, it also proposes them as a new contribution to the theoretical conversation about group development.

As a second example, Steve Barley's (1983) study of a funeral home offers semiotics as a research approach that will allow culture researchers to fully explicate and analyze occupational cultures. He argues that the approach taken so far to surface these meaning systems is not completely up to the task. For example, the study of company logos, organizational stories, and organizational rituals are "but lit candles hovering above both the cake and icing of culture" (p. 409). Again, a metaphor is used to make the point that much of the substance (the cake and icing) of cultural meaning systems is lost by investigative approaches that pay attention only to overtly symbolic phenomena (lit candles); by metaphorically placing at a disadvantage previous research methods (they miss "both the cake and icing of culture"), he distinguishes and advances his theoretical perspective.

As a final example, look at Bob Sutton and Anita Callahan's (1987) characterization of the stigma felt by leaders of bankrupt firms:

> Tom was extremely nervous. He cleared his throat over and over again. He chain-smoked. He was hunched over. His hands and voice trembled. And, he made an odd sort of hissing noise over and over. He looked psychologically beaten. I felt like a voyeur, spying on Willy Loman. (p. 421)

The authors advance a theory about how bankruptcy spoils the image of organizations and of their top managers. The graphic and dramatic portrayal of organization leaders as intensely affected by their company's Chapter 11 status helps to underscore the importance of studying the stigma associated with bankruptcy. This could hardly be better accomplished than by comparing Tom to an almost universally known symbol of personal failure, Willy Loman.

The activity of writing, then, is central to our professional roles as organizational scholars. It is taken for granted that we write in a style that is unadorned and impersonal to allow discovered facts to speak for themselves. This perspective on how we write inauthentically represents what we are about when we write journal manuscripts and only further confounds an already labor-intensive and creative process. In contrast to the prevailing view that stories lay around in some organizational situation waiting to be recorded, we develop the view that the stories we discern in our field experiences have to be authentically crafted and configured. We have to select and develop contextually grounded theoretical points that we present to particular theoretical audiences as offering something new and important to an existing conversation in organizational studies. Only when these audiences have certified the work will our writing have made a contribution to the field.

We now understand that the major task of writing our journals' texts involves working out how to make *contextually grounded theoretical points that are viewed as a contribution by the relevant professional community of readers.* This task involves three components. First, we develop theoretical points that contribute to extant literature. That is, we locate our research within a particular theoretical space, highlight what is problematic, and suggest how our study will resolve that problem. In journal articles, we usually have the opportunity to make one major theoretical point. Second, we contextualize these theoretical points in field-based evidence, emphasizing the primacy of this field evidence in shaping and informing our theorizing. Third, we authoritatively argue the uniqueness of our grounded theoretical points. We marshal our scholarship and particular research to persuade our audience that we have something new to add to an existing theoretical conversation. And we do all of this with our words.

Crafting the Storyline

*H*ow do we, then, make contextually grounded theoretical points that are viewed as a contribution by the relevant professional community of readers? As noted in the introduction, stories provide a narrative structure for incorporating theoretical points into written accounts; stories arrange events and ideas according to their time sequence into beginnings, middles, and endings. In writing up fieldwork, we develop two stories: those based in extant theoretical conversation and those based in the fieldwork. Theoretical stories, the article's macrostory, seek to add something new to the extant conversation in the literature through field-based learnings. Field-based stories seek to bring the theoretical story to life by richly

21

portraying organizational phenomena. They are substories nested within the theoretical story and have their own beginnings, middles, and endings.

Theoretical points, or storylines, are arguments woven throughout the time-based structure of the story that explain differences between beginnings and endings. They are the plots of our stories in organizational studies. We have found it helpful to imagine our articles as nonfiction short stories in thinking about how to make theoretical points. Nonfiction short stories, like our articles, are based on true events and are developed to fit into a small number of pages. In a small space and with attention to portraying truth, nonfiction short stories tell what happened by introducing a complication, showing its development, and disclosing the resolution. The complication is a problem encountered by a person that matters or is troublesome, the development concerns the person's efforts and actions that flow from the complication, and the resolution concerns a change in the person or situation that solves the problem and reduces the tension (Franklin, 1994). The stories that resonate more deeply with readers are those in which real people are confronted with significant problems and, in their journey toward resolving the problem, those real people are profoundly changed (Franklin, 1994).

When applied to our articles, we think of the complication as a problem or an omission that we discern in the literature and that we find significant. The development becomes our depiction of the fieldwork experiences that helped us identify the theoretical complication. Finally, the resolution can be thought of as our proposed change in thinking for that literature that addresses and resolves the complication. Thus a theoretical storyline might read as follows:

In the beginning, the organization studies literature thought x about y. However, y is in reality more complicated than x suggests; x is not the whole story. This richer view of y is important because . . . . Based on this field study, here is what needs to be incorporated into our understanding of y. If we adopt these insights, we can better explain y or see it differently than before.

Our theoretical points introduce a change in our thinking about y (the resolution) that results from the field study (development) and addresses problems (complication) we have identified in that literature. Typically, the introductions of our articles establish the complications and foreshadow the resolutions, the middle sections develop the stories through portrayal of some portion of our fieldwork, and the conclusions examine the resolutions, including the studies' implications for future work. The remainder of this chapter examines how authors, in their articles, construct theoretical points or storylines by discerning problems in the extant literature and resolving them. In the subsequent chapter, we look at the development component of our storyline, which integrates the nested, field-based story.

Crafting Theoretical Storylines

So, how do authors construct storylines? Our own experience is that crafting storylines may be the most difficult, yet most creative, aspect of writing up qualitative research in journal article form. We now believe that storylines do not reside somewhere "out there" in the data or in the literature just waiting to be discovered. If they did, then, as we discussed in Chapter 1, we would just simply write it up. Rather, storylines, we believe, are disclosed through a creative process involving authors, knowledge of relevant theoretical conversations, field experiences, and readers of our work in progress. Storylines emerge, then, from an iterative meaning-making process in which authors simultaneously consider the learnings disclosed in the fieldwork, literature-based conversations, and reader suggestions. Theoretical storylines, and more broadly published articles, are authors' attempts to fully participate in the literature-based conversation by adding something to it.

When we read a published journal article, we are reading the final version of a theoretical storyline, as originally constructed by an author(s) and reconstructed in the review process by some combination of author, reviewers, and editor. What we do not see is how the author arrived at the particular storyline. We do know from our own and others' renderings that finding the theoretical connection for the data seems to occur somewhere in the midst of focused attention and active engagement with our data and the relevant literature conversations. Jane Dutton and Janet Dukerich (1991), for example, share that they discerned the theoretical connection of an article while commuting together. Both remember the scene vividly. They had been commuting together because the nanny for Jane's children was temporarily watching Janet's child. One day, on the way home, they started talking about why the Port Authority got involved with the homelessness issue in spite of clear reasons and incentives for the Port Authority to do otherwise. In the midst of this conversation, they realized that the Port Authority continued involvement with this issue because of the discrepancy between what Port Authority members thought their organization stood for and the picture that the public had of their organization. At this juncture, they both dropped their briefcases and started talking about how this insight shed light on their data. Out of this conversation emerged the conceptual ideas of image and identity. Other times, finding the theoretical connection occurs later in the crafting of our articles. For Karen Golden-Biddle, the theoretical point of a recent article with Huggy Rao (Golden-Biddle & Rao, in press) actually came during the journal review process when one reviewer suggested after the second revision of the initial submission, "The authors have transformed this paper twice—in search of the right theoretical 'hook' that makes sense of the . . . data, while also representing a theoretical addition." This same reviewer suggested that perhaps the concept of identity, a literature mostly unfamiliar to either of them, would shed light on the processes described in the manuscript.

In a recent study, we analyzed how published journal articles using qualitative data established storylines (Locke & Golden-Biddle, in press). We focused, in particular, on the introductions of these articles because this is where scientific work most fully integrates extant theoretical conversations and conveys the proposed contribution. Two key processes emerged from our analyses that, in combination, compose the articles' complications and foreshadow their resolutions. In the first process, constructing intertextual coherence, the articles re-present and organize existing knowledge. The articles variously construe the extant literature as synthesized, progressive, and noncoherent. In the second process, problematizing, these articles subvert the very literature they just constructed that provides the location for the research. They subvert it by identifying a problem variously construed as a gap, an oversight, or a misdirection.

We also found that articles variously connect these two processes of constructing and problematizing the literature. That is, there was not a one-to-one correspondence connecting one particular way of constructing the literature with one particular way of problematizing that literature. Instead, any of the three ways of constructing the literature could be, and had been, connected with any of the three ways of problematizing that literature. Thus we found nine different ways in which storylines had been established.

Process No. 1: Constructing Intertextual Coherence

Intertextual coherence refers to how other related works are configured and referenced in the article so that they relate to each other and to the proposed study. We regard writing the "lit review" to be a major task in setting the scene for the crafting of theoretical points. Consider, for a moment, where we go to find out about a topic; there is no pre-given depository under a "subject" index. There are as many versions of what "the literature" in a given area comprises as there are people writing and reading in that area. To be sure, there is significant overlap, and theorists may agree on what constitute key works in a theoretical domain, but even that is not guaranteed. Certainly, there is not one-to-one agreement on all the works relevant to a topic under investigation.

Consider further that what constitutes the "body of knowledge" is not fixed once and for all by the publication of work. This is a reality with which anyone who has had their work cited is acquainted. Other readers with different understandings of the area or different interests may draw different conclusions and points from the work. Thus a particular work may be disparately relevant to various readers who selectively draw specific aspects of the work.

When we construct and write up our discussion of the extant literature, then, we are doing much more than generating a summary of previous studies and theorizing on a topic. When we construct existing knowledge in a way that highlights the gap that our research will fill, we shape it so that it invites the contribution our work can make. It is as if we configure and reassemble the available pieces of a jigsaw puzzle in such a way that they contour an opening or a space into which our storyline will fit. We rewrite existing work to illuminate the contribution made by our theoretical points.

To illustrate, Karen Locke (1996a) located the contribution of her study on physician-patient interactions in two literatures: organizational emotions and service encounters. To do this, her presentation of related works and relevant citations needed to materialize an intersection between the two research streams:

> The literatures on organizational emotions and service management have an overlapping interest in the affect that occurs in face-to-face encounters between service providers and consumers. For example, much research on

organizational emotions has focused on the display of positive feelings by employees who hold boundary spanning positions in service encounters (Ash, 1984; Hochschild, 1983; Peters & Waterman, 1983; Peven, 1968; Sutton & Rafaeli, 1988; Van Maanen & Kunda, 1989). While, in the service management literature, the display of positive emotions is viewed as central to service providers' roles (Czepiel, Solomon, & Suprenant, 1985; Suprenant & Solomon, 1987) and to the formation of consumer satisfaction (Czepiel et al., 1985; Oliver, 1995; Parsuraman, Zeithaml, & Berry, 1985). (p. 40)

The point of intersection is created by rewriting the literature on organizational emotions to underscore its attention to service encounters and, conversely, by rewriting the service encounter literature to emphasize its concern with emotions. Writing each literature to highlight something that the two had in common, then, constituted a flexible use of them as a resource.

Kilduff's (1993) analysis of *Organizations* indicates that March and Simon (1958) conveniently left out of their discussion of the literature at least two major works that were inconsistent with their indictment of organizational research as subscribing to a machine-like view of human beings. This selectivity allowed them to intensify and press home the predominance of the mechanistic model and set up their own theorizing as a much-needed new perspective. In a different discipline, evolutionary biology, Bazerman (1993) demonstrates the partiality in Gould and Lewontin's (1979) characterization of their literature. In this article, Gould and Lewontin seek to discredit the "adaptationist programme," a broad theoretical framework proposing an adaptive explanation of the survival value of every physical and behavioral feature of a species. To serve their enterprise and highlight the contribution their work makes, they construct the existing literature in evolutionary biology as a struggle between "foolish adaptationism and a wiser pluralism" (Bazerman, 1993, p. 37).

Our point is not that scholars misrepresent the literature to advance their own arguments. Rather, our point is that there is sufficient fluidity and ambiguity in any topical literature to allow it to be authentically interpreted and shaped in a number of directions. Certainly, there are outer limits and norms for constructing literature. But within those limits, there is flexibility in construction. When we examined how authors actually constructed the literature, we discerned three ways: synthesized coherence, progressive coherence, and noncoherence.

Synthesized Coherence

Constructing a synthesized coherence puts together work that previously had been considered unrelated. It highlights the need for new work (e.g., the present study) by disclosing an undeveloped investigative concern that is common to the referenced work. Studies that might otherwise be viewed as unrelated are connected by constructing congruent relationships among the different referenced research streams and studies. The writing of connection between disparate references is evident in comments such as "Despite discrepant pragmatic aims, and regardless of nuances in definition, organizational theorists who write about organizational cultures repeatedly employ key terms that bear a family resemblance" (Barley, 1983, p. 393) and in suggestions that studies of culture are "intellectually akin to a simultaneously growing literature" on organizational symbolism (p. 393). Additional examples of connecting diverse literatures include construing commonality between family theorists and organizational theorists (Hirschhorn & Gilmore, 1980) or relating the work of two authors who studied different topics but which "nevertheless are of considerable interest to the student of intermediary organizations" (Lammers, 1988, p. 441).

Articles construct synthesized coherence in two typical ways. The first one involves the organization of quite discrepant references. In this regard, the article by Bob Sutton (1991) characterizes its intertextual field as reporting "bits and pieces of evidence" on how organizations try to maintain the expression of desirable emotions in light of actors' inner feelings (p. 246). A different article by the same author with coauthor Anita Callahan asserts that "building blocks for a process model of organizational death are to be found in writings on organizational growth and in the sparse literature on dying organizations" (Sutton & Callahan, 1987, p. 542). The second construction of synthesized coherence creates intersections between two or more acknowledged and developed research programs. Illustrations include Steve Barley's (1983) integration of studies of culture and symbolism, Kim Elsbach and Bob Sutton's (1992) blending of institutional theory and impression management literature, and Larry Hirschhorn and Tom Gilmore's (1980) combination of references on structured family therapy and organizational change.

Progressive Coherence

In contrast to synthesized coherence, which relates disparate works containing as yet undisclosed points of intersection, progressive coherence incorporates works already recognized as related in theoretical perspectives and methods. A construction of progressive coherence depicts cumulative knowledge growth over time and consensus among researchers in a well-developed and focused line of inquiry.

Lynn Isabella's (1990) presentation of the literature on the process of organizational change offers an example of progressive coherence. Look at how she writes the literature as gradually filtering toward a need to understand managers' interpretive processes:

> Within the literature on organizational change, there has been considerable research on the sequence of activities that facilitates the process of change (Delbecq & Van de Ven, 1971; Hage & Aiken, 1970; Lewin, 1947; Lippit, Watson, & Westley, 1958). Although change at its most basic level has been said to consist of unfreezing, moving and refreezing (Lewin, 1947), movement through these stages involves more than sequential activities and behaviors. Recent research on selected changes (e.g., Bartunek, 1984; Gephart, 1984; Sutton, 1987) and the literature on organizational change in general have suggested that a substantial amount of cognition and interpretation accompanies the process of change. . . . In other words, as a change unfolds, different assumptions and orientations are required at different times in the process. Managers involved in a change need to undergo an alteration of their cognitive structure (Benne, 1976) that facilitates

and supports the need to change, the process of changing, and the maintenance of what has been changed. The frame of reference—the perspective through which people view an event—shifts (McCall, 1977; Starbuck, 1976). (p. 8)

Beginning with citations that document an interest in the sequence of activities that advance change, the text next moves to works indicating that managers' cognitive processes and interpretive behaviors play a key role in moving through the change process and then ends up with a concern for understanding managers' frames of reference. The literature is written as a setup for the present article, which explicates as a logical next step the study of "the precise nature of these different and changing managerial cognitions and interpretations" (Isabella, 1990, p. 8).

The achievement of cumulative progress often is portrayed through the use of citations. For example, the density of citations underscores that significant research efforts have been devoted to a topic, as in Jean Bartunek's (1984) article on changing interpretive schemes: "(cf. Ford and Slocum, 1977; Hinings, 1979; Bobbitt and Ford, 1980)" (p. 355). Serializing the citations also connotes cumulative progress by showing how successive cohorts of researchers have contributed to a topic. The article by Bartunek continues, "For example, Bobbit and Ford (1980) suggest that an administrator's decision to restructure depends on the administrator's cognitive and motivational orientations" and then moves on to "Ranson, Hinings, and Greenwood (1980) proposed that one of the factors that most affects an organization's structure is . . . members' interpretive schemes" (p. 355). Here, succes-

sive cohorts are shown as contributing to a growing understanding of the relationship between interpretive schemes and
structure.

Noncoherence

In articles constructing noncoherent intertextual fields,
we find referenced works presented as belonging to a common
research program but that are now linked by disagreement. In
contrast to the previous two intertextual fields in which the
construction of consensus was figural, here the focus is on the
construction of discord that, nevertheless, is among researchers who agree on the importance of the research domain. John Langton (1984) and Aimin Yan and Barbara Gray
(1994) provide two examples that construct noncoherent
intertextual fields.

Notice how both articles characterize the field in conten-
tious terms. Langton's (1984) article, for example, claims that
"unfortunately, the relevant literature offers contradictory
assessments" (p. 330), and the article by Yan and Gray (1994)
refers to "continuing controversy in the international joint
venture literature" (p. 1479). This dissensus even extends to
researchers working within the same research program. Thus
Langton (1984) writes,

> *On the one hand, we are told* that "Max Weber was the
> first to consider bureaucracy as the problem of industrial
> society" (Jacoby, 1973:147) that he articulated the "clas-
> sical theory of bureaucracy" (Blau, 1970:14) and that this
> theory, "despite substantial modification and revision,

remains the dominant paradigm for the study of administration and formal organization" (Rudolph and Rudolph, 1979:195; Ouchi, 1980:401-402). All this clearly conveys the impression that Weber's views on bureaucracy constitute as Landau (1972:154) explicitly argued, "a paradigm in Kuhn's sense." *On the other hand, this same literature contends* that all theories of bureaucracy including Weber's are "underdeveloped" (Heiskanen, quoted in Abrahamsson, 1977:36). (p. 330; emphases added)

Similarly, the text by Yan and Gray (1994) portrays dissensus within a literature in the following way: "Research findings on the relationship between control and performance offer conflicting results (see Geringer and Hebert [1984] for a review)" (p. 1479).

Throughout articles constructing noncoherence, we find phrases such as "contradictory assessments" and "continuing controversy" (as in the previous excerpts). Examples include, "no consensus" (Holm, 1995), "competing explanations" (Bills, 1987), and "depressing disputes" (Riley, 1983). Other examples of these internal challenges are seen in depictions of researchers as pitted against each other. Thus Connie Gersick's (1994) text constructs "opposing camps" of researchers on the organizational adaptability issue, locating a group of researchers in each camp. Her earlier work (Gersick, 1988) also writes in such challenges by noting that "Bell (1982) and Seeger (1983) questioned Bales and Strodtbeck's methodology, too" (p. 11). David Bills's (1987) portrayal of three disparate perspectives—"one stream of thought . . . Other writers . . . Osterman is quite convincing that neither interpretation is entirely satisfactory" (p. 203)—points to a research program in disarray.

Developing our theoretical points or storylines, then, relies heavily on first making room in the extant literature for a contribution to be made. Without this gap, the scientific version of a literary trope (Gephart, 1986), there is no room for a contribution to be made; there is no means by which y can be viewed differently before and after the study. But we have seen how our construction of the literature is by no means a given. How we construct it not only shapes and delimits but also acts as a resource for the development of potential storylines.

Process No. 2:
Problematizing the Situation

By constructing the literature, we have set the scene for a contribution to be made through the interplay of the extant literature and the current study. We have situated or located the potential for contribution, not only within a particular topic but also within a particular construction of the related intertextual field. The second process in developing storylines both relies on and complicates this scene. Problematizing the situation not only is grounded in this particular intertextual field but also seeks to problematize that same field and foreshadow the proposed resolution.

Through our study (Locke & Golden-Biddle, in press), we discerned once again that there was not a uniform way in which to problematize an extant literature. Rather, we found three ways: the extant literature as incomplete, inadequate, and incommensurate. Seen as a continuum, as we move across from incomplete through inadequate and on to incommensurate, we find increasing negation and upheaval of that field.

Incomplete

Identifying a gap emerges as the hallmark of an incomplete problematization. When problematizing the literature as incomplete, the article claims that the extant literature is not fully finished; it seeks to contribute by specifying and filling in what is not finished. Thus its complication consists of identifying where further specification is needed in the structured intertextual field, and its resolution is completing that specification. Thus articles problematizing the literature as incomplete seek to refine or further specify existing thinking, x about y. Note how the following excerpt from Bartunek (1984), which constructs the literature as progressive coherence, identifies the gap and specifies the proposed resolution as detailing certain issues not well addressed in extant literature.

> Ranson, Hinings and Greenwood (1980) *proposed that* one of the factors that most affects an organization's structures is powerful organization members' "interpretive schemes." . . . *While [they] make general statements* about the relationships between changing interpretive schemes and restructuring, *they do not address in detail* certain issues pertinent to this relationship. These include the processes by which interpretive schemes change and the means through which such changes are related to restructuring. . . . *The case study supports the Ranson,*

Hinings and Greenwood proposal, but also indicates is-
sues it does not address. (pp. 355-356; emphases added)

An additional example from Kathy Kram and Lynn Isabella (1985) illustrates the identification of gaps in the extant literature that require greater specification. Situated in the mentoring literature, the text complicates this literature by incorporating the notion of "other adult relationships," implying that mentoring relationships are but one type of relationship in work settings important for individual growth. The text fully specifies the gap near the end of the introduction: "Yet, while we know the general importance of relationships, we know little about adult relationships other than the mentoring relationships that directly encourage, support, and contribute to progress in life and career" (p. 112). Here, in one sentence and through the use of the conjunction "yet," the text situates the present work and problematizes the situation.

Inadequate

Illuminating oversights is the hallmark of texts that problematize the field as inadequate. These texts claim that the extant literature does not sufficiently incorporate different perspectives and views of the phenomena under investigation. That is, work in the extant field has overlooked perspectives relevant and important to better understanding and explaining the phenomena. The article seeks to contribute by pointing out the oversight and introducing alternative perspectives and/or frameworks. This problematization stops short, however, of advocating that the extant intertextual field is wrong, preferring instead to allow the proposed alternative framework to coexist with those in the extant field.

In establishing this type of storyline, authors seek to augment extant thought. Thus the construction of the storyline goes something like this:

> In the beginning, the organization studies literature thought x about y. However, x is not the whole story about y. Particular elements such as a, b, and c have been left out. Based on this field study, here are our claims to knowledge about y. By adopting these insights, we can better explain the whole story about y.

Note how, in the following excerpt from Golden-Biddle and Rao (in press), which constructs the literature as synthesized coherence, the article highlights the oversight by suggesting that current research on board functioning (y) emphasizing the economic factors (x) is not the whole story. Cultural elements have been left out. It then foreshadows the resolution by suggesting that the study's findings concerning organizational identity should be used to expand extant thinking about board functioning (y).

> Although there is . . . work on how the functioning of boards is shaped by structural connections . . . political activism . . . and cognitive biases . . . there is no empirical work on how it is influenced by the cultural context. In this paper, we seek to illuminate the cultural embeddedness of boards by examining . . . 1) How does a hybrid organizational identity shape the way board members define themselves and construct their role? 2) What do

board members do when a crisis makes hitherto latent contradictions in organizational identity visible? . . . Our analyses disclose that identity shapes the board role and . . . when a crisis punctures . . . expectations of that role, conflicts of commitment emerge that threaten governance.

An additional example below from Pushi Prasad (1993), which constructs the literature as noncoherent, illustrates the construction of an inadequate problematization by claiming that the literature on computerization and change has overlooked the symbolic perspective of computerization:

> Altogether, a substantial body of research now offers insights into how computers change organizations and into the problems and issues associated with the implementation of computer technology. Yet, some writers (Barry, 1989; Hennestad, 1987) remain dissatisfied with previous work, which they have characterized as incomplete and inadequate. For the most part, they suggest that researchers have . . . neglected the symbolic dimensions of computerized work (Hennestad, 1987; Turkle, 1984). I attempted to fill some of these lacunae by looking at the symbolic processes contained in technological change. . . . This article reports a study of the computerization of administrative operations in a health maintenance organization (HMO) from a symbolic interactionist framework.
>
> Symbolic interaction, an underutilized methodology, has immense potential to augment scholarly understanding of organizations. . . .
>
> More recently, a theoretical recognition of the symbolic nature of computers and information technology has gained strength. Turkle (1984) . . . pointed out the computer is an extraordinarily evocative technology,

holding different meanings for different people. Perhaps the most seminal piece of work in this genre is Feldman and March's (1981) article identifying the symbolic nature of information and information technologies in organizations as providing "ritualistic assurances" of managerial competencies. Further, Hennestad (1987:141) suggested that "computers and their systems also play a role as metaphor and source of ideas" . . . and Brissy (1990) described the "magical" symbolism of the computer in the workplace.

Despite this theoretical recognition of the significance of the symbolism of computerization, very few empirical studies have systematically documented it or explored how it can influence organization-level action. . . . Such a perspective could, however, clearly offer considerable insights into the processes of computer implementation in organizations. (pp. 1400-1402)

Note how the text sets up the oversight by referencing authors within the field who "remain dissatisfied with previous work" and in particular with how that work has "neglected the symbolic dimensions of computerized work." In this same paragraph, which is the second paragraph of the published article, the text also positions itself and its author with the group of writers who are dissatisfied with extant literature.

What is perhaps most interesting is how it builds the case for the alternative perspective through the use of adjectives and adverbs that introduce a partisan viewpoint. For example, when the text points out how the alternate perspective can redress the oversight, it does not simply suggest this and move on. Rather, it argues strongly for the benefits of adopting such a perspective. Accordingly, the text announces that this perspective has "immense potential," not merely potential. Furthermore, this perspective could not just add to the literature, it "could . . . clearly offer considerable insights." Finally, when referencing literature as support for the alternate perspective, the text once again invokes descriptors that move away from a neutral depiction. Thus we see supporting research as representing a "theoretical recognition of the symbolic nature of computers" that "has gained strength." This literature "points out" that "the computer is an extraordinarily evocative technology, holding different meanings for different people." Although the tone remains polite and generally upholds neutrality, a partisan viewpoint is nevertheless explicitly introduced by positively depicting the alternate perspective.

Let us take two final examples of inadequate problematizations. The first example, by David Thomas (1993), constructs the literature as progressive coherence, whereas the second, by Dutton and Dukerich (1991), constructs it as synthesized coherence. Consider, as you read, how they both illuminate oversights in the extant literature and foreshadow how they will address that problem.

> In the past several years, race relations has continued to grow in importance as a topic of academic interest. It is now recognized that despite gains made since the 1960s, racial inequalities persist. . . . Yet organizational research has rarely focused on the dynamics of interracial work-centered relationships and thus has offered little to advance our understanding of the influence of race on organizational processes. . . . Little research has been done on developmental relationships in racially integrated workplaces that examines how these relationships

> work. This paper addressed that issue. (Thomas, 1993, pp. 169-170)

What is the storyline proposed by Thomas? Before reading on, take a moment to frame what you perceive as his storyline.

To us, his storyline reads as follows. During the past few years, the subject of race relations and research on race relations (y) is increasing in importance (x) "as a topic of academic interest." However, important aspects of the story on y have been left out of most studies. In particular, "little research has been done on developmental relationships in racially integrated workplaces." This study's findings will provide a more comprehensive rendering of the influence of race relations in work organizations.

Next, examine the article by Dutton and Dukerich (1991). Again consider the following questions. What is their storyline? How do they complicate the extant literature and what sort of resolution do they propose?

> Models of how environments and organizations relate over time have typically assigned causal primacy to either environmental or organizational forces. . . . None of these theories treats in depth the processes by which environments and organizations are related over time. . . . In this research, we developed a framework for conceptualizing the process through which organizations adapt to and change their environments. . . . Our claims were built from a case study. (pp. 517-518)

What perspective are they suggesting has been overlooked, and what needs to be incorporated into the study of organizations and environments?

Incommensurate

The hallmark of articles that construct an incommensurate problematization is their direct advocacy for an alternative thesis that is better than those put forth in the extant literature. Whereas we need to closely examine articles with an inadequate problematization to discern partisanship, in these articles that partisanship is explicitly conveyed. In this respect, problematizing the literature as incommensurate goes further than inadequate problematizations by claiming not only that the extant literature overlooks different and relevant perspectives but that it is wrong, misguided, or incorrect.

In contrast to refining or augmenting the extant literature, articles that problematize the literature as incommensurate seek to reformulate or redirect that literature. The storyline goes something like this:

> In the beginning, the organization studies literature thought *x* about *y*. However, *x* is misleading, wrong, or significantly incomplete. Based on this field study, here is what should be said about *y*. If we adopt these insights, we can redirect our thinking and better explain *y*.

Note how the following two excerpts from David Boje (1991) and Kathy Eisenhardt (1989) challenge the thinking of the extant literature.

Arguing that stories examined in previous research on storytelling have been "wrenched from their natural performance contexts," the article by Boje (1991) advocates for the alternative thesis that storytelling be studied as a dynamic process that occurs within a specific performative context.

Clearly, the word "wrench" is not a neutral word. According to the *Oxford English Dictionary*, the word denotes forcible movement and can mean to force out of the right way. The right way is the study of storytelling in its natural performative context; previous research has gone away from the right way, the wrong way.

The article does not begin with the word "wrench" and the head-on challenge to the extant literature. Rather, it first asserts the advantages of seeing storytelling as a dynamic process in context, and only later does it insert the challenge. Note how the following excerpt depicts the elements of dynamic process and stories as performed in an organizational context, so crucial to the proffered alternative perspective:

> In organizations, storytelling is the preferred sense-making currency of human relationships among . . . stakeholders. People engage in a dynamic process of incremental refinement of their stories of new events as well as ongoing re-interpretations of culturally sacred story lines. . . . Even in stable times, the story is highly variable. (Boje, 1991, p. 106)

Soon after, the article marshals prior literature and citations— other than the one challenged—to support the alternative thesis. It declares,

> The important fact is that most storytelling is done in conversation and involves the listeners. . . . Some socio-linguists have analyzed how conversations happen and, in a few studies, how conversations are told. . . . Harvey Sacks (1972a, 1972b) and his followers (Sacks, Schlegoff, & Jefferson, 1974; Jefferson, 1973, 1978; Ryave, 1978)

have investigated the contexted occurrence of stories in conversation. (p. 107)

Note how, through the insertion of the word "fact" and scientific references, the text elevates the alternative perspective of storytelling in context to truth. At the conclusion of this section, just prior to the direct challenge, the article claims that these more "complex aspects of storytelling in organizations" have been "ignored" by organizational analyses of story.

Up to now, the problematization of the situation could be categorized as inadequate, although the article certainly provides clues to the developing incommensurate problematization. It still has the opportunity to construe an inadequate problematization; in this case, the storytelling process in context is an alternative perspective that deserves to be studied and to be incorporated alongside other perspectives. However, in the very next sentence and the subsequent 112 lines of the article, the direct challenge of the extant literature on storytelling is made explicit:

> Stories in previous laboratory, history and questionnaire research generally have been wrenched from their natural performance contexts and treated as objectified social facts (Ritzer, 1975), mere texts, with little empirical attention given to the natural linguistic context in which the stories are being performed. Text research does not capture basic aspects of the situated language performance. . . . In case history studies, researchers have relied on second- and third-hand accounts of a story rather than examining a storytelling event in process. . . . In the case of lab study research, performance skills are not a consideration. . . . The transition from the lab to the organiza-

tion is fraught with difficulties. . . . Story-text studies relying on interview methods have also ignored performance behavior. . . . Finally, in the case of surveys, the textual content rather than the storytelling event is the focus of study. . . . Such an approach does not tell us about how those stories were performed in their natural elements. . . . It is not a behavioral analysis of in situ performance. . . . Stories can therefore be correctly interpreted only to the extent that the researcher grasps the story in situ. (Boje, 1991, pp. 107-109)

Through the use of the word "wrench," the use of questions to challenge the reality of prior research results, the continual juxtaposition between prior research and the proposed alternative, and the insertion of the words "situated," "real," "in situ," "natural," "performance," and "context," this text mounts a direct challenge of the extant literature and advocates strongly for its own alternative thesis. It does not want to just coexist with that prior work; it wants to overthrow it and replace it with the proposed perspective. Finally, it pronounces, with no attached reference, "Stories can therefore be correctly interpreted only to the extent that the researcher grasps the story in situ." The strong implication is, of course, the judgment that research conducted on stories out of context is incorrect.

The article by Eisenhardt (1989) is our second example of an incommensurate problematization. Arguing that the prior research on rapid strategic decision making does not deal with "two key realities," this text advocates for an alternative thesis bolstered by empirical findings that challenge the traditional literature. Specifically, the article suggests that "extant views may inaccurately describe how executives make rapid decisions" (p. 544).

Once again, this article does not begin with the challenge but rather builds up to it as the introduction unfolds. The article begins with a story of failed decision making in a context demanding speed and indicates that this story is "not unusual." Then, it identifies an oversight of the prior literature—"There has been little research on fast strategic decision making" (Eisenhardt, 1989, p. 544)—and invokes citations to legitimate the existence of this oversight. Immediately thereafter, the text identifies the proposed contribution of this study: "This article explores the speed of strategic decision making. . . . The empirical grounding of those ideas is the subject of this article" (p. 544). Up to now, the storyline—both the complication and the proposed resolution—has been portrayed matter-of-factly and with humility, portraying neutrality in line with scientific norms (Gephart, 1988; Knorr-Cetina, 1981). However, sandwiched between these neutral sentences is the essence of this text's incommensurate problematization.

Consider, as you read, how this article constructs an incommensurate problematization of the literature. What specific language helps to convey that the literature is misguided or wrong?

> This article explores the speed of strategic decision making. . . .
>
> The results reported here are a set of propositions challenging traditional views of strategic decision making. The evidence suggests that fast decision makers use more, not less, information than do slow decision

makers. They also develop more, not fewer, alternatives. In contrast to current literature, this study found that centralized decision making is not necessarily fast, but a layered advice process emphasizing input from experienced counselors is fast. The findings also indicate that conflict resolution is critical to decision speed, but conflict per se is not. Finally, integration among strategic decisions and between decisions and tactical plans speeds, not slows, decision making. Such integration helps decision makers cope with the anxiety of high-stakes decision making. Overall, fast decision making allows decision makers to keep pace with change and is linked to strong performance. A pattern of emotional, political, and cognitive processes that are related to rapid closure of major decisions emerged from this research.

The empirical grounding of those ideas is the subject of this article. (Eisenhardt, 1989, p. 544)

What is your reading of how the article constructs an incommensurate problematization?

Ours is that it mounts a direct challenge of the extant literature and advocates very strongly for its own thesis. Specifically, Eisenhardt (1989) points out that her findings demonstrate that executive teams make rapid decisions differently from what the literature would presuppose. However, because the challenge is sandwiched between neutral-sounding statements and because it rests on "findings" and "evidence," the challenge still is cast critically but politely. Nevertheless, through the constant juxtapositioning between prior research and the proposed research findings, a linguisitic device prevalent in this construction of problems in the literature, this article actively provocates and advocates for its own thesis. In a very real sense, it uses existing theory as a foil to highlight the contrast between findings.

In crafting our storylines—the theoretical points woven throughout our stories—we find it helpful to imagine our articles as nonfiction short stories, each composed of a complication, a development, and a resolution. In this chapter, we examined two processes—constructing intertextual coherence and problematizing the literature—that authors use to construct the theoretical complication and foreshadow the resolution. The presentation of intertextual coherence identified the conversation the study proposes to join. At the same time, its problematization highlights the unique contribution made by its theoretical points.

Developing
the Storyline

*I*n Chapter 2, we examined how authors craft theoretical storylines by finding problems in the extant literature (complication) and resolving them (resolution). In this chapter, we delve into how authors develop their storylines through their contextualizations in field data. In journal articles, the development of a storyline occurs primarily, although not exclusively, in the middle section. Consisting of a field-based story nested within the structure of the theoretical story, the central purpose of development is to take readers "there"—to transport them into the field—and to bridge the worlds of the field and the readers. We take readers into the field by conveying the vitality of everyday life encountered in the field; we bridge the worlds of the organizational members, authors, and readers by connecting the field life to our theoretical points.

To transport the readers into the field, articles need to portray the researchers' firsthand experience with the organization members' world. The authors employ their acquired familiarity with everyday life in all of its cognitive and affective fullness to vividly convey the members' experience to readers (Golden-Biddle & Locke, 1993). However, efforts to take the readers into the field are, at the same time, pointing to the readers' world and to the theoretical points being advanced in the articles. For example, when we choose to incorporate data, we do so with an eye toward not only showing the everyday life in an authentic manner but also providing evidence for our theoretical points. Or, when we vividly and dramatically portray the lives, predicaments, and feelings of organizational members, we again point to and shape our theoretical points. Portrayal of life in the field vindicates our theoretical points as it concretizes them in particular organizations. The data thus provide excerpts of organizational life that readers can take, on the one hand, as representations of particular persons or situations studied and, on the other, as concrete expressions of theoretical points being advanced in the articles. In this chapter, we describe how authors variously incorporate field data to develop their storylines.

Enlivening Beginnings:
Developing the Storyline in the Introduction

Interestingly, the depiction of details about everyday life in organizations often is introduced in the very beginning of the article. These opening lines and sections are crucial elements in the establishment of rapport between the work and its readers (Law & Williams, 1982). The conventional "abstract" remains. However, following the abstract, a number of authors are choosing to delay their consideration of the literature in favor of a "sneak preview" of the organizational context analyzed. They do not choose just any details of the organizational life to portray; they choose those that begin to develop the storylines that will be explicitly articulated later in their introductions. Thus the beginnings of a number of journal articles based on qualitative studies are taking on a different look. Bob Gephart's (1993) introductory paragraphs in his study of risk and blame in disaster sense making read as follows:

> **Gas Blast Blamed on Wind Shift**
> A sudden shift in the wind may have triggered a spectacular pipeline explosion that critically injured five Big City men Tuesday night. The gas in the high-pressure 51-cm pipeline was probably ignited by equipment brought in to repair a leak, says [the] director of operations for the Western Pipe Lines. (newspaper article, February 20, 1985)

Foreman Was a Family Man

[Western Pipe Lines] (Ltd.) lost a 30-year employee when Merv Ginter died in the burn unit of University Hospital Monday. But to the members of his family, Ginter's death represents the loss of a husband, a father and a grandfather. (newspaper article, March 5, 1985)

Pipeline Worker Dies

[A second] of five pipeline workers injured in an explosion died Wednesday. (newspaper article, March 7, 1985)

Public Inquiry Testimony

In light of the serious nature and tragic consequences of the leak, the Board is holding this public inquiry into the accident. The purpose of this inquiry, therefore, is to permit the Board to determine whether any changes should be made in the way that [Western Pipe Lines] operates or the way in which [it] is regulated by the Board, in order to prevent similar accidents in the future; it is not the primary purpose of this inquiry to fix any blame for what happened. (chairperson of government energy board, March 26, 1985) (pp. 1465-1466)

Rather than taking readers to the literature, this beginning transports them directly to the context of the study: the pipeline explosion, sense making about risk management, and the allocation of blame subsequent to the explosion.

Similarly, Jane Dutton and Janet Dukerich's (1991) study of organizational image, impression management, and adaptation begins with this paragraph:

> The homelessness problem is perhaps a blight on that professionalism that we like to display, and that we are so proud of, and I think this is of great concern here. Again, there may be some conflicting issues on spending money to help solve the problem, but I think that's a value. We build beautiful facilities, we take pride in that, and the homelessness issue is something that obviously affects the perceptions of us. (facility staff member, Port Authority of New York and New Jersey, 1989) (p. 517)

Readers are immediately taken to listen in on the comments made by an organization member of the Port Authority of New York and New Jersey as he expresses his concerns about the organization's image ("perceptions of us") and interest in whether the organization will respond/adapt ("some conflicting issues on spending money to help solve the problem").

A final example is presented in the opening to Kathy Eisenhardt's (1989) study of decision making in high-velocity environments. Time and decision making, the central elements in this article's storyline, are foreshadowed in a number of ways:

> In October, 1984, Gavilan Computer filed for bankruptcy protection under Chapter 11. Despite a $31 million stake from venture capitalists, Gavilan experienced delays and indecision that ultimately cost the firm its early technical and market advantages. The firm's leading-edge technology became a "me too" one and competitors flooded its empty market niche. As the firm died, one executive mourned: "We missed the window." (p. 543)

Time is referenced in the "delays" experienced, in the change of its leading-edge technology into a "me too one," and in the executive's lament that they had "missed the window." Decision making is indexed in the "indecision that ultimately cost the firm."

Taking readers to the field in the first lines of the article not only piques their curiosity that "real" and interesting organizational situations will be portrayed but also provides them with an orienting glimpse into the storyline that will be developed.

Providing Explanatory Information: Novel Use of Methodology Sections

Every story needs to give readers enough background information so that they can understand the context of events or statements. Given the short space of journal articles, an interesting development is the growing use of the methodology section to provide information on the organizational setting essential to understanding the events portrayed. Given the contextual nature of qualitative research, authors have, in essence, reshaped the methods section to augment the development of their storylines.

For example, Karen Golden-Biddle and Huggy Rao (in press) subdivide their "Research Methodology" section into "Research Setting," "Data Collection," and "Data Analysis." In the "Research Setting" subsection, the article details the founding of Medlay as well as the formal structure and functions of the board of directors. The information on the board not only conveys details of Medlay but also lays the ground-work for showing how organizational identity shapes board member interactions and the enactment of their role more than does formal role.

Brian Pentland (1992) subdivides his "Method" section into "Research Setting," "Access and Observation," and "Data." His discussion of research setting begins,

> A hot line is a convenient setting in which to study service performances because the work consists of large numbers of discrete units . . . that are processed fairly routinely. Lave (1988) argued that everyday, routine activities of this kind are especially appropriate topics for practice theory. (pp. 533-534)

This article argues that knowledge is situated performance and that practice theory can provide the conceptual foundation for this view. Here the discussion of the research setting advances the theoretical point by claiming that a hot line in a software organization is the appropriate setting in which to study routine and develop a theory about knowledge as situated performance.

A final example is that of Debra Meyerson (1994), in which she subdivides the "Methods" section into "Informants and the Research Settings," "Data Sources," and "Analysis." Her study analyzes interpretations of stress and, in particular, examines how ambiguity and burnout are culturally produced by hospital social workers. This theoretical perspective weaves throughout the entire Methods section. As an example, we focus on the "Informants and the Research Settings" sub-section:

I studied social workers because their work is in many ways ambiguous (Huntington, 1981; Ehrenreich, 1985). Here, ambiguity refers to a general lack of clarity. . . . Burnout, following the literature, refers to emotional strain and exhaustion. What is significant here, however, is what these concepts mean to participants.

Members of this occupation report high degrees of stress and are highly prone to burnout (e.g., Cherniss, 1980). Social workers face ambiguity in their technologies (e.g., talking to clients), their goals (e.g., to provide empathy and caring), their evaluation criteria (e.g., sensitivity), and occupational boundaries (e.g., who is and is not a social worker). I situated the research in hospitals because hospitals are embedded in strong institutional (versus technical) environments (Meyer and Scott, 1983).

To understand how institutional processes constrain social workers' understandings and behaviors, I studied social workers who performed in comparable tasks in organizations embedded in different institutional environments. (pp. 632-633)

Showing and Telling: Data-Theory Coupling

In our journal articles, the data never stand on their own. No matter how "detailed and accurate" the fragments of organizational life reported in manuscripts are, their theoretical implications are never left for readers simply to take. Conveying data looks in two directions; backward to the research situation to the forms and processes of organizational life encountered there and forward to the theoretical points to resolving problems identified in the literature. Underscoring this relationship between depicting data and conveying their theoretical meaning, the literary critic, Wayne Booth, distinguishes between "showing" and "telling." He explains that the "accumulation of accurately observed detail cannot satisfy us for long; only if the details are made to tell, only if they are weighted with a significance," do they hold our attention (Booth, 1961, p. 114). We both show data and tell their significance. We theorize the fragments of life we show. Consequently, in our manuscripts, we couple the fragments of organizational life with our theoretical points and commentaries. The life we portray always is theorized as, reciprocally, the theory we develop always is contextualized.

However, authors face choice points in developing their storylines, most of which center around the ordering of showing and telling and the proportion between showing and telling. Although the vast majority of authors lead with theory in journal articles, they arrange and compose their theory telling and data showing in different ways. Moreover, even within the same article, authors do not necessarily stick with just one way of telling and showing; they may vary it in light of their particular data and storylines.

Telling, Showing, and Telling

Some authors develop their storylines using a sandwich structure; they first explain how the theoretical point will be evidenced in the subsequent data, then show that data, and finally tell what the data showed. For example, in this excerpt from an article by William Kahn (1993), we are first told about and then shown the nature of caregiving that flows between a social worker and her client in a social service agency:

> Other aspects of the flow pattern are highlighted in the following excerpt of a phone conversation between a social worker and her client, a mother of four boys. The care that the social worker gave her client was a rich concentration of each of the dimensions of caregiving. She made a lot of time available to the woman, patiently inquired about and attended to her story, showed respect and empathy for her effort and struggles, supported her with information meant to empower her to take control of her life, and offered such care consistently during the conversation. Her end of the conversation included this passage:
>
> > *I called to see how things are going. I'm glad you're able to use this phone at work. How are the matches going? [Listens] Good. I'm glad. How did you feel about that? [Listens] You sound like you handled that well. [Listens] I'll get back to you about the free shoes we have. I definitely have you in mind and will start to have a bit more time. Were you able to apply to some of the housing projects I sent you information about? [Listens] I'll keep my eye out and when I see things I'll send them to you. [Listens] You have to remember to do something for yourself. With four kids and another 100 at the day-care center during the day, you have to do something for yourself. Get together with other people, adults at the center. Make that a priority.*

This passage shows the social worker patiently listening and inquiring into her client's experience, making room for the woman to be present emotionally ("How did you feel about that?") and concretely ("Were you able to apply?"). (pp. 548-549)

In this example, Kahn begins with telling by detailing the characteristics of caregiving that flow between social workers and their clients. He follows this up with showing when he enacts and materializes those characteristics in the presented phone conversation. He returns at the conclusion of the excerpt to telling in his translation of the caregiver's behavior into theoretical terms. The distinction between telling and showing is further highlighted by the article's switching into a different font as the author changes from narrating the theory in the voice of the organizational scholar to demonstrating it in the voice of an organizational actor and then back again.

A second example, by Connie Gersick (1988), proposes a midpoint transition as a critical development event in work teams:

The Midpoint Transition

As each group approached the midpoint between the time it started work and its deadline, it underwent great change. The following excerpts from transitional meetings illustrate the nature and depth of this change. Particular points to notice are members' comments about time and their behavior toward external supervisors.

Excerpt 5(E5) The students begin their meeting on the sixth day of an 11-day span.

1. Rajeev: I think, what he said today in class—I have, already, lots of criticism on our outline.

What we've done now is OK, but we need a lot
more emphasis on organization design than what
we—I've been doing up till now.

2. Jack: I think you're right. We've already been
talking about [x]. We should be talking more
about [y].

3. Rajeev: We've done it—and it's super—but we
need to do other things, too.

4. (Bert agrees.)

5. Jack: After hearing today's discussion—we need
to say [x] more directly. And we want to say more
explicitly that.

6. Rajeev: Should we be organized and look at the
outline? We should know where we're going.

(The group goes quickly through the outline members
had prepared for the meeting, noting changes and additions they want to make.)

7. Rajeev: The problem is we're very short on time.

It is significant that Rajeev's remark, "We're very
short on time," was only the second comment about the
adequacy of the time the group had for the project, and
it marked a switch from Hack's early sentiment that
"we've got some more time" (E2,6). A new sense of
urgency marked this meeting. (p. 23)

As was the case with the social work example, Gersick begins
by making a theoretical point; the development of work teams
is characterized by a midpoint transition. Then, before pro-
ceeding to bring that midpoint transition to life by showing its
enactment in a particular work team, she directs readers to
"notice" the elements of that transition, time, and change (in
their behavior toward authority) in the fragment of team life

she presents. Having shown the data of team life, she once again calls readers' attention to the element of time and, in so doing, underscores and advances the theoretical framework.

Minimal Telling, Showing, Telling, and More General Telling

Other authors develop their storylines by immediately showing data (usually after a subheading that signals theory) and then telling the theoretical significance of that data after they have been shown. These showing-telling episodes then build into a more general discussion of theory (telling) that is demarcated in the text as a separate section. However, this more general telling section still is distinct from, and often immediately precedes, the final section of the article, that is, the discussion or conclusion.

Our first example is by Golden-Biddle and Rao (in press). The first empirical section of the article, "Medlay's Organizational Identity and the Role of the Board," seeks to establish the theoretical point that a hybrid organizational identity, consisting of being volunteer driven and being a family of friends, shapes the board role in this organization. This section is divided into the following three subsections: "Medlay as a Volunteer-Driven Organization," "Medlay as a Family of Friends," and "How Identity Shapes the Board Role." Note, in the following excerpt of the first two paragraphs of "Medlay as a Volunteer-Driven Organization," how the authors minimally tell through the heading of the subsection and then show an extended quote. Finally, they end with telling, that is, linking the data to the concept of identity, their theoretical concept.

Medlay as a Volunteer-Driven Organization

"Reflecting the broader American culture within which it exists, Medlay prides itself in encouraging broad volunteer participation and strong volunteer governance. . . . One of the most often stated, yet least understood, parts of our culture is that Medlay is a volunteer-driven organization. Ultimately, the only truly unique part of our culture is that volunteers govern our destiny. This concept and principle is sacrosanct and must be preserved for us to be fully accountable to the public and to our mission statement. Obviously, since we are a large organization, it is essential that we employ and retain highly skilled professional staff. However, it is critical that the volunteers not relinquish their responsibility."

This excerpt, delivered to board members and management by the Board Chair . . . portrays a central, distinctive and enduring belief in Medlay as a volunteer-driven organization. The middle portion of the Board Chair's statement most clearly delineates the importance of this belief.

This subsection and the one titled "Medlay as a Family of Friends" represent the showing-telling component of developing the storyline, that is, how the board role is shaped by the different and conflicting aspects of the organizational identity. The third subsection, "How Identity Shapes the Board Role," represents the more general telling component of developing the storyline and, most explicitly, bridges the data to the theoretical point by developing a model of how identity shapes the board role.

Another example of this form of coupling data and theory is the article by Dutton and Dukerich (1991). This article examines how individuals and organizations make sense of and enact "nontraditional and emotional strategic issues" using the particular issue of homelessness. A dominant portion of their empirical portrait, then, concerns showing how the issue of homelessness changes in interpretation over time. The section titled "Interpretations of and Actions on Homelessness" depicts five chronological phases distinguished by key events, major interpretations, and major actions regarding the homelessness issue. The data are both discussed in the text and summarized in a figure depicting the history of the homelessness issue. In the subsequent section, "The Role of Organizational Identity and Image," the authors develop the more general telling component of the storyline, linking it to relevant literature.

Our final example is Gephart's (1993) study of disaster sense making. In a section titled "Analysis," this article shows the data: individual stories of the disaster by the assistant district manager, the worker, the district manager, and the board. These stories are conveyed more thoroughly in the accompanying tables. The stories are developed in the text, primarily by showing transcribed data verbatim, although some telling enters near the end of each story in reflective comments about the data made by the author. However, the telling explicitly begins with the subsection titled "Key Words" in which conceptually related clusters (e.g., rules and policies, safety) are developed from a textual analysis of the transcript data. Finally, the more general telling is found in a separate section following "Analysis" titled "Summary of Findings."

Theoretical points alternate with data to document and make concrete the conceptualization proposed by the researchers. The proposed theoretical frameworks depend on the data, and the organizations and actors they symbolize, to support and demonstrate the conceptualizations in "real life." Conversely, the data depend on the theory to give them relevant meaning in light of the extant literature. Furthermore, each acts as a constraint on the other. The theoretical framework shapes readers' apprehension of the data, and the data provide the form for the theory. This interlocking of data and theory reinforces the coherence of our storylines, giving them the quality of straightness.

Portraying Data to Capture the Drama and Vitality of the Field

Looking over the qualitative articles appearing in journals, we noticed that the glimpses into organizational life that they afford often are vivid and quite dramatic. That is, the organizational circumstances and the data fragments through which they are portrayed convey compelling human stories.

Portraying Dramatic Moments

As cases in point, consider these very dramatic moments in individual and organizational careers that inform our theorizing in organizational studies. One of the more striking examples is provided by Karl Weick (1993), who seeks to advance our understanding of organizational sense making through analysis of a forest fire:

> Two people, Sallee and Runsey, made it through a crevice in the ridge unburned. Hellman made it over the ridge burned horribly and died at noon the next day. Dodge lived by lying down in the ashes of his escape fire, and one other person, Joseph Sylvia, lived for a short while and then died. The hands on Harrison's watch melted at 5:56, which has been treated officially as the time the 13 people died. (p. 629)

Analogous accounts of disasters are provided in Barry Turner's (1976) analysis of failures of foresight involved in three major disasters in Britain and Gephart's (1993) analysis of sense making following a gas pipeline explosion that resulted in the deaths of two men and severe burns to a number of others. Highly dramatic and intense moments of organizational life such as those present themselves with a sense of urgency. Authors theorize these moments to inform and provide practical avenues for possible intervention.

Other examples come readily to mind. Jerry Ross and Barry Staw (1993) advance theory about organizational escalation from their study of the construction of the Shoreham Nuclear Power Plant, a project that "turned into a bet-the-company" proposition (p. 716). Diane Vaughan (1990) discloses the organizational contribution to technical failure, in particular in the *Challenger* tragedy, by analyzing how monitoring and regulating processes failed to identify flaws in management procedures and technical design. Bob Sutton and Anita Callahan (1987) build theory about the consequences and management of spoiled identity in the context of the career-ending consequences of Chapter 11. As one senior manager in their fieldwork commented, "I think it's the equivalent of having accidentally killed your spouse and then having to live with it for the rest of your life" (p. 421). Kim Elsbach and Bob Sutton (1992) advance theoretical points about organizational impression management through their analysis of the actions of two organizations, EarthFirst! and Act Up! Members of these organizations engage in illegal actions because of the environmental and personal stakes they understand to be at issue. For members of Act Up! who suffered AIDS symptoms, it is a question of "fight or die." For members of EarthFirst!, it is the life of the planet that is in jeopardy: "As EarthFirst!'s founder, Dave Foreman, put it: We're sticking a wrench in the system, we're slowing it down, we're thwarting it, we're kicking it in the face!" (p. 703).

Portraying Vital Moments

In an analogous way, many of the data fragments in our manuscripts portray more mundane, yet nevertheless vital, moments encountered in the field. How do we retain in our writing the vitality of these situations as expressed in the field?

As authors, we have available to us our vast field data, often reaching hundreds and even thousands of pages. Which of the hundreds of collected experiences and stories do we select to write into our texts? Edmonson (1984) points to the need for selectivity in the choice of exemplars of organizational life to be included in our writeups. These "condensed examples" should not only illustrate the theoretical points but also embody vividness that brings the points alive in a way that evokes the human interest of readers. The examples should draw readers into the organizational situations studied and invest them in the storylines developed. Thus authors choose the most vital moments experienced in the field, or the singular most expressive comment, to take readers full tilt into their stories while illustrating the theoretical point being offered.

Consider these examples in which data fragments disclose vital moments in everyday life experienced by organization members. These too are used to convey theoretical points. They take readers to the situation and bring home the theoretical points in a particularly visceral way. Consider Karen Locke's (1996a) examples of comedic encounters enacted in an outpatient clinic examining room:

> Dr. Roberts finishes an examination of a 13-year-old young man who, following 5 years of dialysis, has had a kidney transplant and is doing well. He begins wrestling with him on the examination table and jokes about taking him back, "Now the dialysis girls said they'd have the machine ready for you." Josh, laughing and wrestling back, yells out insistently, "Nooo!" Roberts continues his exaggerated threats. He pushes Josh back down on the examining table, "Lie you down," he playfully punches him in the stomach, "Make you puke." Again, Josh howls out, "Nooo!" Between the laughter. Mother is watching and laughing along. (p. 52)

Consider Eisenhardt's (1989) example of an executive facing a situation in which his management team has just rejected his idea for developing an IBM-compatible product:

Frustrated by his rejection and facing an impending deadline, the CEO came up with a new alternative. Without consultation, he made the choice himself. As he stated, "I said to hell with it and shoved it down their throats." (p. 564)

Consider Anat Rafaeli and Bob Sutton's (1991) illustration of how both positive and negative emotional strategies are symbolically expressed in the good cop there and the bad cop outside:

After a few hours, I was as tight as a spring. Even when I was with the good cop and the bad cop was outside, I couldn't relax. I feared that any moment he would walk in and start going crazy. (p. 267)

Consider David Boje's (1991) example of storytelling in a storytelling organization, Walt Disney productions, during its founder's years:

Frustrated by the noise of a lawn mower outside the conference room window, Harry, a Disney executive, opened it and yelled at the top of his voice. "Shut off that goddamned machine and get the hell away from here, you stupid son-of-a-bitch!"

The roar of the power mower stopped abruptly. Once again, all was quiet. The Disney executives resumed their meeting.

Ten minutes later the session was interrupted again by a phone call. It was [Walt] Disney. His tone was stern. He ordered Harry to come to his office "at once."

"Harry," Walt growled, appraising him, "I understand you just raised hell with one of my gardeners."

"I'm sorry Walt," Harry shifted uneasily. "I guess I lost my cool."

Walt glared at him. "That old man has been with me twenty-two years," he snapped, "and if I ever hear of you cussing him out again—I'll fire your ass." (p. 126)

As a final example, we glimpse into an intensive-care unit cubicle where a 6-month-old baby has been receiving chemotherapy (Locke, 1996a):

> Dr. Morris physically examines, then, standing in silence with both hands resting on the crib rail, looks intently at the baby, Brian. [Pause] He switches his gaze to Mom and Dad, standing beside each other on the opposite side of the crib. They are silent, their gazes fixed on their son. Dr. Morris's eyes move back and forth between the baby and Mom and Dad. (The silence persists.) He looks better, asserts Dr. Morris, looking at Mom and Dad. [Pause] His voice now softer and more tentative, he asks, "Does he look better to you?" Dad says nothing. Mom sighs and shrugs her shoulders. Their eyes haven't moved from their son. (p. 53)

Passages such as these, and the ones highlighted throughout this chapter, develop their storylines by providing vivid illustrations of organizational life. They take the readers to the field. We feel our emotional response as we read about disasters, homelessness, bankruptcy, and other compelling human conditions. We are transported to the field, absorbing its vitality. But we do not stay there. Rather, the better storylines cohere so completely that they interweave field and theory, letting each inform and illuminate the other. The authors craft unique theoretical points that are contextually grounded and that seek to achieve a seamless rendering of theory and data.

Characterizing the Storyteller

Let us begin by taking a brief excursion to ancient Greece—to one of the Platonic dialogues. Here we find Socrates about to deliver a speech that challenges the arguments posed by a young man, Phaedrus, in an address just delivered on the subject of love. Socrates is in somewhat of an awkward position. He finds the arguments he must make in his speech to be morally offensive. Consequently, in anticipation of the words to follow, he declares, "I shall cover my head before I begin; then I can rush through my speech at top speed without looking at you and breaking down for shame" (quoted in Hamilton & Cairns, 1961, p. 237). Although Socrates is delivering an oral speech as opposed to offering a written text, the image of him covering his head and dashing through his presentation allegorically points to two significant dimensions of characterizing the storyteller in our work: how authors portray themselves in their work and whether or not audiences regard this portrait of authors as consistent with their expectations.

Socrates' actions first direct our attention to the author's character as a central aspect of any discourse, whether it is spoken or written. The text Socrates is about to deliver is one from which he would prefer to dissociate himself; however, the image of the shrouded speaker only highlights the relationship between Socrates and, in this case, his spoken words. Similarly, in the act of racing through the words, almost as if trying to escape them as they fall from his lips, Socrates actually reaffirms the connection between author and text. Second, Socrates references the audience, "you," to whom he directs his speech. In both oral and written discourse, an audience is established. The obvious difference is that in written discourse that audience is implied; authors neither see the readers nor engage them in face-to-face interaction. Nevertheless, a particular audience is imagined, and authors in part shape their character in the text according to what they think this implied audience views as acceptable and trustworthy. What we are asserting, then, is that authorial character always is constructed by authors in the text, even in our "scientific" journal articles. To build on Socrates' example and paraphrase the literary critic Booth, authors never can choose to vanish completely from their texts; they can only pick the disguise in which they will appear.

The preceding discussion of Socrates, implied authorial character, and implied readers takes us to the thesis of this chapter: that, in various ways, intentionally or unintentionally, we express a character in our written accounts. This does not mean, however, that only one type of character is crafted. As we will see, although the institutional scientist is the dominant character crafted in journal articles, the degree and intensity of this character varies. In addition, within the institutional delimitations, some authors shape their character by persisting in a particular style over time or by departing more markedly from the way in which typical journal articles are crafted. In this chapter, then, we are concerned with how authors express themselves in journal articles, and we organize our discussion by first depicting the character of the institutional scientist and then by examining how some authors distinguish themselves as individual scientists.

Storyteller as Institutional Scientist

When seeking to publish in organizational studies journals, we need to establish characters that are recognized and regarded as credible by our readers. In these journals, the implied readers are reviewers, editors, and other colleagues in the discipline. These readers have been trained in the conduct and philosophy of science through extended professional schooling and often have conducted work in similar areas. Thus they come to the reading of our manuscripts or articles with particular points of view regarding topic and with internalized norms for conducting science. Geertz (1988) forcefully makes the point about this relationship between authorial character and reader receptivity, insisting that authors' abilities to establish themselves as part of their readers' particular disciplinary community is basic to getting their manuscripts published, read, and cited.

The issue of depicting a reader-receptive character more specifically faces researchers who rely on qualitative data. As Glaser and Strauss (1967), Strauss (1987), and Strauss and Corbin (1990) point out repeatedly, qualitative work will be read, and most likely evaluated, by those who use quantitatively based research methodology. This situation is rapidly changing, however, as greater numbers of researchers using qualitative data are now ad hoc reviewers, editorial board members, and/or editors. This points, perhaps, to a situation in flux where authors develop the character of institutional scientist in their work but do so with less adherence to traditional canons associated with work based on quantitative data. Consequently, we expect to find some variation in how the institutional scientist is depicted.

We find, consistent with the use of a "scientistic" style in academic writing as documented by McCloskey (1994), that qualitative work does portray the storyteller as a scientific character and thereby inserts the mark of the institution. Accordingly, we portray ourselves as "scientists at work" by conveying objectivity and technical competence. In addition, and unique to researchers who collect data close up *in* organizations, we find that conveying field knowledge also is a significant dimension of portraying the storyteller as scientist. Borrowing from ethnographic work in anthropology and sociology (Golden-Biddle & Locke, 1993; Van Maanen, 1988), authors show that they have "been there" and that this experience has allowed them to understand and interpret organizational phenomena in a different, but equally scientific, way. Let us look at the way in which we depict each of these three characteristics of the institutional scientist in our work.

Institutional Scientist as
Objective Storyteller

Representing the style of no style, or windowpane prose discussed in Chapter 1, an objective storyteller appears to be telling the story as it really happened (McCloskey, 1990, 1994). This storyteller conveys the story as if it were a straightforward rendering of the facts with minimal personal involvement. The data are constructed as independent from any authorial influence or bias. After reading the manuscript or article, the readers are left with the impression that anyone could have gone into the field and come out with similar findings (Van Maanen, 1988).

Conveying independence from the data creates a special issue for qualitative researchers because we have entered the field and relied on ourselves as the major data collection instruments. We intentionally use a methodology that enhances our involvement with the phenomena we study. The question we face, then, in writing journal articles is as follows:

Do we convey—and if so, how do we convey—the requisite institutional objectivity and yet remain true to the different type of data we collect?

Data as Evidence

A major way in which we establish objectivity, and thereby convey the character of the institutional scientist in our work, is by presenting data as evidence of our theoretical points. As evidence, the data acquire the ontological status of "factual statements" (McCloskey, 1994); they are presented as if they originated from a source other than the author and represent opinions of persons other than the author. For example, we rarely use personal pronouns in the data sections, presenting the data as if they were collected independently. Moreover, we employ data as evidence to support, substantiate, and advance our theoretical points.

When writing up qualitative research for journal articles, we construct data as "evidence" in at least four distinct ways. First, some authors format the data differently in the text so that they stand out more readily from the analyses. For example, some authors use quotation marks or indent and single-space their data. In a number of articles published in *Administrative Science Quarterly*, a smaller font size is used for the presentation of verbatim data. This practice helps readers discern quite easily what organizational members said from the interpretations drawn by the authors. Consequently, the trail of authorial logic between data and interpretation is more apparent.

Second, a few authors explicitly assess the strength of their data for readers. For example, they categorize the types of data provided to support their theoretical points according to whether it is "strong" or "modest" evidence. In particular, some authors use the following notation in their work: I = strong evidence from interviews, i = modest evidence from interviews, O = strong observation evidence, o = modest observational evidence, and so on. When data are arrayed and categorized with such weighting, the result conveys that there is overwhelming and impressive evidence to support the theoretical points. We would like to issue a caution, however, concerning the practice of weighting data. When weighted, qualitative data convey an objectivity and quantifiable preciseness that, we believe, are impossible and undesirable to obtain. In a recent discussion with Bob Sutton, one of the authors who has used weighting, he noted that, although weighting helps him analyze data, he now regards its use in articles as depicting "false rigor" that perhaps is inserted to "make quantitative researchers happy." In essence, weights wrap qualitative data with quantitative trappings and, in so doing, not only signal to reviewers that the work should be judged on quantitative terms but, more important, obfuscate the more subtle meanings that could be disclosed in more completely arraying the data.

A third practice is to place data in tables distinguished from the textual discussion. Tables help authors to more succinctly convey additional data as evidence of theoretical points. And they assist the readers' task of discerning data from author interpretation. Furthermore, our experience is that more and more reviewers, including ourselves, are requesting the development of tables. However, although such tables are very useful in orienting readers and in efficiently showing the vast amounts of data we collect, they also can signify the data as separate from the storytellers. Tables convey the impression of letting the data speak for themselves by presenting them in tabular form, lined up and ready for reader inspection (McGill, 1990). So, although tables are useful, they should be crafted with care and integrated into the textual discussion.

Finally, some authors seek to directly establish the objectivity of their data and thereby contribute to an objective characterization consistent with the expectations of scientific readers. Take the following illustrations:

> We understood the biases we brought to the research as individuals and as a team. We could, therefore, take care to minimize the impact of our biases on the data collected. (Kram & Isabella, 1985, p. 115)

> The basic facts of the Shoreham case are objectively verifiable. . . . The size of Shoreham's losses (see Table 1) and the set of events leading up to this disaster are not . . . in dispute. Finally, evidence on the independent variables . . . was assembled from multiple sources, many of whom were arms-length observers of the phenomenon. (Ross & Staw, 1993, p. 708)

A special case of constructing data as objective evidence arises when authors rely on someone else's accounts to make their theoretical points. In these cases, the data sources for the study invite the attribution of contamination. Karl Weick's (1993) article on the Mann Gulch disaster comes to mind because, in developing his theoretical points, Weick relies exclusively on a secondary data source, Norman Maclean's (1992) book, *Young Men and Fire*. Look at how, in the following excerpts, he justifies as evidence the use of this data source. The justification begins in the final sentence of the very first paragraph of the article, "I want to strip Maclean's elegant prose away from the events in Mann Gulch and simply remove them to provide a context for the analysis" (p. 628). In seeking to convey objectivity, the author inserts his own prose, "strip away" and "simply remove them." Later, he uses two and a half pages to detail the methodology that was used by Maclean to write the original book. Concluding this section, Weick comments, perhaps in anticipation of or in response to reviewer challenges,

> If these several sources of evidence are combined and assessed for the adequacy with which they address "sources of invalidity," it will be found that they combat 12 of the 15 sources listed by Runkel and McGrath (1972:191) and are only "moderately vulnerable" to the other three. Of course, an experienced woodsman and storyteller who has "always tried to be accurate with facts" (p. 259) would expect that. The rest of us in organizational studies may be pardoned, however, if we find those numbers a good reason to take these data seriously. (p. 632)

The irony, of course, in depicting ourselves as objective storytellers is that, in so doing, we illuminate how we use language (e.g., facts, verifiable, data, arms-length observers) to achieve this portrait. We are not suggesting that our scientific products are invalid or otherwise unscientific. Rather, we are making the point that they are constructed with language within the context of the institution of science (Gusfield, 1981; Knorr-Cetina, 1981; Latour & Woolgar, 1986).

Institutional Scientist as Technically Competent Storyteller

In addition to establishing objectivity, as authors we seek to portray ourselves as technically competent storytellers by telling how we have adhered to particular canons for the conduct and analysis of our research. The question for qualitative researchers in organizational studies has been as follows: To which canons do we adhere, those traditionally associated with quantitative research or emerging ones associated with qualitative research? Our own preference is to adhere to canons that are most authentic to qualitative research.

In reading qualitative work, we have observed technical competence conveyed through adherence to either quantitative or qualitative canons. Sometimes we have found adherence to both sets of canons in the same article! Both sets of canons have in common the goal of systematically collecting and analyzing data. How they define "systematically," however, differs. Let us look first at quantitative canons of technical competence. Consider in the following illustrations the use of language and criteria normally associated with quantitative research:

> To ensure the accuracy of the category coding, I had an independent reviewer, blind to the purpose of the research, code some data. (Isabella, 1990, p. 13)

For example, when a set of nonequivalent dependent variables is predicted and found to result from a particular treatment of process, an investigator can be relatively confident that such an effect has indeed occurred. Likewise, if a consequence is predicted and found to result from a particular array of nonequivalent independent variables, a strong inference can similarly be made. (Ross & Staw, 1993, p. 705)

The study used a multiple case design that allowed a replication logic, that is, a series of cases is treated as a series of experiments. (Eisenhardt, 1989, p. 545)

Other authors develop their technical competence by justifying qualitative research on its own ground. Consider in the following illustrations how language signals the use of different criteria:

The empirical research was designed as a series of interpretive case studies, performed in 1984-1987. We asked the respondents to describe the history of the reorganizations from their own personal experiences and perspectives. Historio-graphical . . . methods . . . were used to balance the various, sometimes conflicting, perspectives against each other. In qualitative investigations, versions of the same course of events often differ radically. . . . Historians have elaborated methods to handle this problem by carefully analyzing and weighing against each other several factors relating to distortions of the written or oral sources. (Skoldberg, 1994, pp. 220-221)

Throughout the research, our goal was to increase the dependability of the data . . . a type of contextual validity (Diesing, 1971) that is concerned with understanding the human system in its particularity to the extent possible from the members' perspectives. Dependability enables the researcher to assert that a certain uniformity exists in the data collected . . . and that the resulting interpretations authentically and plausibly, though not with absolute certain or accuracy . . . explain what was researched. (Golden-Biddle & Rao, in press)

During the research I became filled with many of the emotions (e.g., anger, sadness, joy) that members experienced. . . . I used a journal and clinically trained colleagues to help me reflect on my experiences, learn about the issues involved and work through emotions that threatened to undermine my capacity to collect further data. (Kahn, 1993, p. 543)

Ironically, regardless of which approach authors adopt to justify their work, most reference the work of Glaser and Strauss (1967), which has acquired the status of "exemplar" guidance for conducting qualitative research. Not only do authors parenthetically cite the work by Glaser and Strauss, but in some cases they write this exemplar work into the main body of the text. This latter practice demonstrates more vividly for readers that the storytellers are technically competent because they are following solid and established methodological practices and procedures as laid out by reputable intellectual predecessors and contemporaries.

The goal of the process, which followed the recommendations of Glaser and Strauss (1967) . . . (Rafaeli, 1989, p. 251)

The analysis procedure followed the grounded theory approach formulated by Glaser and Strauss (1967) and more recently employed by several others. (Isabella, 1990, p. 12)

This method draws on descriptions of how to generate grounded theory by Glaser and Strauss (1967). (Elsbach & Sutton, 1992, pp. 705-706)

To develop the conceptual framework presented here, we followed the procedures for building grounded theories outlined by Glaser and Strauss (1967), and subsequently refined by both authors. (Locke & Golden-Biddle, in press)

As writers and readers of qualitative work, we would like to issue a cautionary note with regard to the citing of so-called exemplar work; however, in sounding this caution, we want to make clear that we believe Glaser and Strauss (1967) is a fine work to cite and have done so in our own work as well. But on more than one occasion while reviewing manuscripts, we have been left with the impression that these names have become a sort of "boilerplate" justification for qualitative research. The problem with boilerplates, as we see them, is twofold (Locke, 1996b). First, authors begin to reference this work without themselves having any real understanding of the underlying ideas. In some cases, we suspect that the authors have not read even parts of the original work but are taking others' renditions of the "grounded theory" or "theoretical saturation" ideas developed by Glaser and Strauss. When we invoke these or other ideas without particular knowledge, we really are using them only for the stamp of approval to legitimize our work. Essentially, we invoke these references as an impression management device vis-à-vis our reviewers so as to have our work "bask in the reflected glory" of another (Gilbert, 1977). Furthermore, without reading the originally developed work, we lose the particular contribution of the original work as we rewrite its general meaning into our own work.

Second, by relying so much on a few references, we miss the diversity of what constitutes qualitative research. Qualitative research constitutes a sizable umbrella under which there are many traditions. By not knowing the work we cite, we may insert references that actually offer contradictory viewpoints on how qualitative research should be conducted. Accordingly, we confuse the methods of investigation that have been developed and create an impression that "anything goes" in the conduct of qualitative research.

Institutional Scientist as Field
Knowledgeable Storyteller

An obvious and unique characteristic of qualitative research is that it is field based. The very act of contextualizing our theoretical points in field data automatically raises the questions of whether we "were there" and, if we were there, whether we were able to experience enough to allow us to understand and interpret what went on. Following the lead of anthropologists and others doing ethnographic research (Van Maanen, 1988), we often rely on the "have been there" authority to characterize ourselves as scientific in our work.

Did we observe and record in sufficiently fine detail to warrant an insightful and competent understanding of the situation studied? As we indicated in previous work (Golden-Biddle & Locke, 1993), when authors portray a detailed familiarity with the field setting and its members, they are establishing themselves as authentic or field-knowledgeable storytellers. That is, as authors we convey certain details and understandings of the field obtainable only by having been there. In that earlier research, we identified three types of field knowledge that authors convey to establish that they were in the field.

First, when authors use insider language to depict theoretical points, they not only concretize the proposed theory but also underscore that the storytellers have achieved intimate familiarity with organization members' lives. The use of colloquialisms by Patricia Adler and Peter Adler (1988) in their description of the resocialization of basketball players—a key component in their framework for developing intense loyalty—illustrates this:

> No players, even the "candyasses," were immune from these tirades [from the coach].
>
> They were no longer high school stars. . . . Instead they were freshmen, "riding the bench," waiting their turn. . . .
>
> The coach drilled the individualistic "hot dog" qualities out of them and shaped them into team players. (p. 407)

Second, by portraying familiarity with members' actions, what they do every day, authors also establish their field-knowledgeable character. William Kahn (1993), in his study of caregiving in a social service agency, details eight behavioral dimensions of caregiving that, he notes, "were often inter-woven together in daily interactions" (p. 545). By showing these interactions in detail, as illustrated in the following excerpt, he established his knowledge about the field:

> For example, when a new social worker presented a difficult case, a senior social worker listened patiently, asked probing questions, withheld judgment, validated the other's efforts by saying how impressed she was with the sensitivity and judgment displayed, empathised with the other's struggles by sharing her sense of the frustration and sadness she sensed from the other, and supported the other by offering feedback about how she was framing the case in a constraining way. (p. 545)

Finally, when authors portray what members think about their lives in particular organizations, they also establish their field-based expertise. In the following illustration taken from a study of funeral home workers, Steve Barley (1983) reveals the staff's innermost thoughts and fears about their work, that is, that they do not want to drop the body as it is being moved from the home to the funeral parlor:

> Having positioned the onlookers away from the scene, the funeral staff moves whatever furniture is necessary to provide open access for the litter, but the path is also cleared to assure that no unwanted noise might be caused by bumping the stretcher into pieces of furniture. Noises are avoided in order to guard against, among other things, the perception that the staff has dropped the body. (p. 407)

Storyteller as Individual Scientist

When we orient our work to journal publication outlets, all of the work we examined, including our own, develops the character of institutional scientist. However, within these institutional delimitations, some authors shape their character to depict their individual mark on the scientist role. When the character of individual scientist is very sharply crafted and, in particular, distinguished from the institutional character for that type of publication, authors are recognized in the writing, even when their names are not visible. For example, Geertz (1988) discusses the highly personalized styles of eminent anthropologists as portrayed in books, Evans-Pritchard's highly visual "slide show" style being a case in point. In this respect, the creation of an individual character becomes the "writer's characteristic way of saying things" (Morner & Rausch, 1991, p. 214) or more the person in the writing. Thus individual character often is demarcated by the way in which it is distinguished from the more typical character in its genre.

Authorial Persistence

The first way in which the individual scientist is depicted in organizational studies journal articles is through what we call authorial persistence. In this case, authors continue, over time, to use one particular way of writing up their research. Although still very much illustrative of the institutional scientist, the authors differentiate themselves as individuals through their persistence; over time, they are recognized in the work from the way in which they write it up.

For example, think back to Chapter 2 when we examined the two processes used in crafting storylines. Authors first construct the intertextual field as synthesized, progressive, or noncoherent and then problematize that field as incomplete, inadequate, or incommensurate. When authors publish multiple articles and construct the same storyline in all of them, they distinguish themselves as individual scientists in their work. Let us take three examples.

Steve Barley is differentiated in his work through his use of an incommensurate problematization. Remember that those articles problematizing the literature as incommensurate directly and negatively challenge alternate perspectives; in some cases, alternate perspectives are seen as rivals whose privileged status must be dethroned. In both his earlier work on semiotics (Barley, 1983) and his more recent work with Gideon Kunda that we excerpt in the following (Barley & Kunda, 1992), he challenges directly extant thinking:

> This paper challenges the prevalent notion that American managerial discourse has moved progressively from coercive to rational and, ultimately, to normative rhetorics of control. . . . Although the thesis of a progressive shift toward normative control has considerable elegance, it rests on a reading of history that underplays events in the late nineteenth century and that ignores streams of thought that gained prominence after World War II. Rectifying these oversights warrants a different interpretation of the historical record. . . . Rather than having evolved linearly, managerial discourse appears to have alternated repeatedly between ideologies of normative

and rational control. . . . Consequently, at least in broad contour, the history of managerial thought appears less a progression than a continued wrestling with counter-punctual themes. (pp. 363-364)

Connie Gersick (1988, 1994) is differentiated in her work through the creation of a storyline that incorporates a nonco-herent literature field and an inadequate problematization of that literature. Constructing a noncoherent literature, authors reference works that are presented as belonging to a common research program but that are linked by disagreement. An inadequate problematization signals that the current literature overlooks key perspectives or views. Note, in the following excerpt, how Gersick (1994) combines both processes to construct such a storyline:

> A major controversy of the past decade of organization theory centers on adaptability. . . . One camp, associated with theorists such as Aldrich (1979), Hannan and Free-man (1977, 1984), Leberson and O'Connor (1972) and others, stresses the difficulty, rarity and liabilities of or-ganizational change and the weak impact of managerial choice on organizational outcomes (e.g., Pfeffer and Sal-ancik, 1978). Theorists such as Child (1972), Barnard (1938) and Miles and Cameron (1982) anchor an oppos-ing camp, arguing that managers can make consequential choices that keep their organization adaptive and aligned with changing demands. . . . The emerging findings offer support for both sides. . . . The accumulating evidence argues that research might well begin to focus less on "do they or don't they" and more on when and how organi-zations steer successfully through changing environ-ments. (pp. 10-11)

Finally, Bob Sutton is differentiated in his work by the construction of the literature as synthesized coherence. Remember that synthesized coherence is characterized by the integration of multiple yet previously unrelated streams of research to bring to attention different topics of inquiry. As illustrated in Chapter 2, Sutton (1991) has characterized one study's intertextual field as reporting "bits and pieces of evidence" from a variety of literatures (p. 246). Similarly, in another article with Callahan, the "building blocks for a process model of organizational death are to be found in writings on organizational growth and in the sparse literature on dying organizations" (Sutton & Callahan, 1987, p. 542). Finally, in his work with Elsbach, they explicitly integrate institutional theory and impression management literature to examine issues of organizational legitimacy (Elsbach & Sutton, 1992).

Crafting the Atypical

The second way in which authors distinguish themselves in their work is by crafting storylines that are atypical for journal articles. In the vast majority of journal articles that we examined for a recent study (Locke & Golden-Biddle, in press) and for this book, authors crafted storylines in which complications were based in extant literature and field data were used to provide a context and evidence for theoretical points. Thus the articles theorized the field stories; theory was figural and data were important, although secondary.

The work by Barry Turner (1976), "The Organizational and Interorganizational Development of Disasters," departs from the typical construction of the storyline; it not only theorizes the story, it also stories the theory. Let us examine in greater detail what that means. In the following excerpt, look at how Turner (1976) constructs a field-based complication, which we italicize:

> Administrative organizations may be thought of as cultural mechanisms developed to set collective goals. . . . Given this concern with future objectives, analysts have paid considerable attention to the manner in which organizational structures are patterned to cope with unknown events—or uncertainty—in the future facing the organization and its environment (Crozier, 1964; Thompson, 1967; Lawrence and Lorsch, 1967).
>
> Uncertainty creates problems for action. Actors' organizations resolve these problems by following rules of thumb, using rituals, relying on habitual patterns, or, more self-consciously, by setting goals and making plans to reach them. . . . But since organizations are indeterminate open systems, particularly in their orientation to future events (Thompson, 1967:10), members of organizations can never be sure that their present actions will be adequate for the attainment of their desired goals.
>
> Prediction is made more difficult by the complex and extensive nature of the tasks. . . . When a task which was formerly small enough to be handled amenably grows to an unmanageable size, resources may be increased to handle the larger problem . . . (Hirsch, 1975). . . . Alternatively, the task to be handled may shrink to fit the resources available or the amount of information . . . (Meier, 1965). . . . The success of these strategies, however, turns on the issue of whether the simplified diagnosis of the present and likely future situation is accurate enough to enable the organizational goals to be achieved

without encountering unexpected difficulties that lead on to catastrophe.

The central difficulty, therefore, lies in discovering which aspects of the current set of problems facing an organization are prudent to ignore and which should be attended to, and how an acceptable level of safety can be established in carrying out this exercise. (pp. 378-379; emphasis added)

This complication is grounded in real life; it consists of a real-life problem that members of a variety of organizations find significant. Which problems should be attended to so that we can avoid catastrophe? This complication matters and, in so doing, places the field context central and figural to the article. To bring home the theoretical importance of this issue, Turner (1976) incorporates relevant literature on uncertainty into his discussion. Note, however, that he does not yet problematize the extant literature; rather, he uses it as relevant context for the field-grounded complication. In this respect, he stories the theory.

Turner (1976) then proceeds to construct the theoretical complication, which is derived from the field complication:

Wilensky (1967) has suggested that to deal with such situations, one must discover how to recognize high-quality intelligence about the problem at hand, using the term intelligence in its military sense. Wilensky's criteria for high-quality intelligence are that it should be "clear, timely, reliable, valid, adequate and wide-ranging." . . . This is excellent as a normative statement of what is desirable, but it does little in practical situations to offer tests of clarity, timeliness, or adequacy of intelligence. One means which Wilensky did put forward for tackling these latter issues, however, is by the examination of failures of intelligence, these being more important than failures of control. Taking up this suggestion, this article considers the manner in which such an approach could be used to begin to identify, as Wilensky (1967:121) puts it, "the conditions that foster the failure of foresight." (p. 379)

This time, the complication is grounded in the extant literature and in particular in the work of Wilensky. However, the theoretical complication does not leave the field behind; this time, it is used as a context of relevance for the theory. Indeed, the theoretical complication is grounded in how it helps "practical situations." Thus Turner's storyline embodies two central, figural complications—one based in the field and the other in the literature—and implies that resolutions will be developed for both. These complications are so integrally interwoven that it is difficult to discern where one begins and the other ends.

Finally, Turner (1976) develops an added twist to his complications; that is, he complicates the complications and, in so doing, renders them more significant and important for both the organizational members and academics. Specifically, and clearly, he first defines the type of disasters that he will examine as those that "present problems of explanation" and continues as follows:

The concern, here, therefore, is to make an examination of some large-scale disasters that are potentially foreseeable and potentially avoidable, and that, at the same time, are sufficiently unexpected and sufficiently disruptive to provoke a cultural reassessment of the artefacts and precautions available to prevent such occurrences. The intention of this examination is to look for a set of patterns that precede such disasters. Having identified such a pattern, one can go on to ask whether it can also be found in the preconditions for other major organizational failures which do not necessarily lead to loss of life, but which, nevertheless, provoke the disruption of cultural assumptions about the efficacy of current precautions, such as the collapse of a public company. (p. 380)

Both organizational members and researchers want to continue reading to gain insight on how to prevent disasters and organizational failures. Does he develop patterns and, if so, what are they? It is this insight into disasters, if disclosed, that resolves the significant complications.

Importantly, we believe that by constructing a story based on both field and theoretical complications, Turner (1976) opens up his work to his readers. It has the potential to resonate and find a home with not only an academic audience but also the managerial audience. And he does this without sacrificing any academic insight.

The discussion in this chapter of characterizing the storyteller explicitly raises the question of how we represent ourselves in our writing. By distinguishing between the institutional scientist and the individual scientist, we have illustrated how, as members of our profession, we construct both uniformity and uniqueness in our writing. Thus our writing choices both emerge and multiply as we become increasingly conscious of how we and others convey the storyteller in journal articles.

5

Rewriting the Story

*W*hat happens to the stories we tell when we submit them to journals for peer review? How do our stories change in this formal review process? What roles do the institutional gatekeepers, namely reviewers and editors, play in rewriting our stories?

To explore these questions, we spoke with several authors who graciously took the time to be interviewed and provide us with the written "traces" of their particular review processes: original submissions, revised drafts, reviewer and editor comments, and the authors' responses to the reviewer/editor comments. Their generosity has made it possible for us to look at the institutional passage of "Stories of the Storytelling Organization: A Postmodern Analysis of Disney as 'Tamara-Land' " by David Boje (1995), "Keeping an Eye on the Mirror: Image and Identity in Organizational Adaptation" by Jane Dutton and Janet Dukerich (1991), "The Textual Approach: Risk and Blame in Disaster Sensemaking" by Bob Gephart (1993), "Irony and the Social Construction of Contradiction in the Humor of a Management Team" by Mary Jo Hatch (in press), and "Maintaining Norms About Expressed Emotions: The Case of Bill Collectors" by Bob Sutton (1991). To these, we have added the histories of our own works, "Breaches in the Boardroom: Organizational Identity and Conflicts of Commitment in a Non-Profit Organization" by Karen Golden-Biddle and Huggy Rao (in press) and "A Funny Thing Happened: The Management of Consumer Emotions in Service Encounters" by Karen Locke (1996a). In this chapter, we share some basic themes we found in our analyses of the conversations and written materials.

Manuscripts Differently Engaged Reviewers and Editors

An interesting aspect of these authors' experiences of the review process is that although all of the studies clearly engaged the reviewers and editors, they did so for different reasons. For example, one of Bob Sutton's (1991) reviewers was especially curious about the study's setting, credit rating companies. This reviewer commented,

This paper offers a fascinating view into a world often regarded as mysterious and intriguing. In our current society, the prediction that Big Brother would be watching us has often come to be translated into the activities of the credit rating companies, with their expansive reach into nearly complete knowledge of our activities. These bill collectors form one arm of that gigantic system.

Furthermore, the editor highlighted this interest in the cover letter:

As the reviewers remarked, this is a fascinating peep into the workings of a mysterious occupational curiosity—the bill collector. And while the show doesn't have quite the elegance of A Taxing Woman, the material is reasonably detailed and provocative.

Similarly, the consulting editor on Jane Dutton and Janet Dukerich's (1991) study of how the Port Authority dealt with the issue of homelessness remarked, "The reviewers of the paper are very attracted to the issues you are addressing . . . and to the empirical setting which you have selected to study the problem." In reflecting back on her experience of the review process, Janet Dukerich remarked on how "the issue of homelessness was emotionally engaging for the reviewers." In the case of Karen Locke's (1996a) paper, the descriptions of comedic behavior seemed to engage one reviewer, who remarked, "I am particularly impressed with the intuitively appealing descriptions of the microperformances and the author's ability to choose strong examples that bring to life the meaning that might be assigned to these observations." In contrast to the preceding examples, for Mary Jo Hatch's (in press) article, it was the theoretical framing of her study that was interesting to the reviewers, one of whom wrote, "I am intrigued with the idea of examining a discursive style—irony to explore action in conditions of high uncertainty and to gain access to the 'organizational underside.' " Finally, in the case of David Boje's (1995) article, the editor remarked on a personal interest in the study of Disney: "I found the general story of Disney leadership to be interesting. Perhaps this is because I grew up at a time when Disney was 'king.' Furthermore, the general historical data and background are interesting."

Thus the reviewers were engaged by the studies' views into inaccessible settings, portraits of compelling human issues, detailed microviews of behavior, and foci on irony to access invisible aspects of organizing, the person of a leader, and so on. However, on a final note, not all reviewers needed to be engaged by the study for the editor to make a "revise-and-resubmit" decision. It was enough for at least one or two readers to be engaged by a study, even if for different reasons.

Reviewers and Editors Requested Often Substantial Changes

An intriguing dilemma created by the reviewers' and editors' engagement with a study is that, on the one hand, the engagement leads to their support for the studies whereas, on the other, that same engagement evokes greater involvement in suggesting changes to the manuscript. Engagement with the manuscript seems to predispose reviewers to want to become involved with, and to actively participate in, directing the revision of the work. With the exception of Bob Sutton's (1991) article, whose editor strongly directed the revision, all of these papers went through at least two major revisions before final acceptance. The work by David Boje (1995) underwent five revisions.

As noted in a recent study by Beyer, Chanove, and Fox (1995), a characteristic of manuscripts receiving revise-and-resubmit decisions is that reviewers get actively involved in trying to improve them. Thus we cannot be sure that the extensive involvement we see with these papers is any different from that with papers based on quantitative data. Nevertheless, we suspect that there are differences in types of changes requested in light of some of the authors' comments and the multivocality of qualitative data (a point we discuss in the next section).

In the requests for often substantial changes to the manuscripts, the basic credibility of these research endeavors never was at issue. Rather, the reviewers regarded the studies as works in process and the central responsibility of their role as providing "the author with direction for enhancing" the informative value of the works to the organization studies community (Rousseau, 1995, p. 152). This responsibility is particularly evident in the "Eye on the Mirror" article (Dutton & Dukerich, 1991), the paper in this group that changed the least. From the original submission, it was clear that the editor and reviewers viewed the manuscript favorably. This was evident in comments such as "your rather lovely paper" and "I enjoyed your paper." Indeed, the editor characterized the original submission as having established the basic foundation for the paper. Even with these very positive responses, the paper nevertheless went through two more revisions, which the editor described as directed at developing and strengthening what already had been accomplished in the original submission.

Although the review process is directed at highlighting and strengthening journal articles' information value and significance to the community of organizational scientists, and although the authors noted how helpful the review process was in further strengthening their manuscripts, such involvement has a potential downside for authors. The level of involvement by reviewers in the paper by Karen Golden-Biddle and Huggy Rao (in press) caused Huggy to comment one day that, in qualitative research, the reviewers in effect become "coauthors." Taking this comment even further, David Boje commented at the end of his interview, "I don't think it's my paper anymore. It is group writing. I'm just one of the players." Finally, Bob Gephart noted that although the reviews were helpful, "Every time I wrote something, it got unwritten."

Some of the authors identified how the reviewer engagement with their works led to particular tensions during the process. First, a few authors noted that because different reviewers were engaged with different aspects of their works, the reviewers sometimes proposed revisions that were quite distinct, or even incompatible, with each other. Although the editors of these manuscripts stepped in to help resolve any differences and provide direction for further revision, because the reviewers were so engaged, the authors risked writing out of the text what had originally engaged reviewers (and other potential readers).

Second, and more typically in this group, authors noted that there were instances in which reviewers and editor comments actually took the manuscript revision further away from what the authors originally wanted to say. For example, tension surfaced when the stories the authors wanted to tell were different from those that reviewers and editors believed an audience of organizational scholars would be interested in reading. Bob Sutton explained that, in his revision, the editor strongly urged him to move in one direction, a direction that moved away from his own original interest in conducting the study. Instead of examining the influence of emotions on behavior, the editor requested that he examine norms about the expression of emotions.

> The paper seems to pursue several goals at once. . . . All but the first of these has little to do with organizations per se. . . . We recommend that you take a firm choice about one of these themes and forget the others for the sake of this presentation. Our own recommendation is that you pursue the theme outlined in the first paragraph and focus it with the noted question [i.e., How does an organization seek to determine the display of an agent's emotions when the agent is simultaneously subject to influence from his own emotions and from his client's behavior?].

In a different vein, Janet Dukerich noted that even though "Eye on the Mirror" is her "most favorite paper," she feels that the story of the Port Authority started "to become sterile" as less and less of the field story remained through the revisions. Finally, Bob Gephart indicated that he felt a responsibility to the widows and family members of the men who had died to tell the story that the idea of organization itself is a myth. His story was redirected away from that and toward the methodological contribution because he had submitted his manuscript to a special research methods issue. By stepping into the writing of the manuscripts, the reviewers and editors participate in the rewriting of narrowly focused, coherent theorized stories that they believe will provide the most new information for their journals' audiences. However, these stories are not always the same ones that authors most wanted to tell.

Rewriting Through the Review Process: How the Manuscripts Changed

With regard to specific changes requested by editors and reviewers, not too surprisingly, their suggestions for change focused on the theoretical positioning of the studies and on the theoretical significance of the data, not on the data themselves. We suggest that this is not surprising for two reasons. First, as developed in Chapter 1, disciplinary readers in science, such as those in organizational studies, are primarily interested in details or facts provided by our data only as illustrations of theory or points of view (Langer, 1964). It is their significance that matters—their significance to the theoretical conversation. Thus the questions become the following: What do the data mean, and what import do they signify? It is these questions that are in most dispute and on which the reviewers and editors focus most of their comments and suggestions.

The second reason for the focus on the theoretical significance and positioning of the data is that qualitative data are multivocal. They can point to one of a number of possible theoretical explanations and thus have implications for a number of theoretical conversations (Campbell, 1975; Gephart, 1978). The reflections of a reviewer on Karen Locke's (1996a) findings underscore just how multivocal our data can be in terms of their relevance for various theoretical conversations. This reviewer commented,

> However, there are available empirical findings as well as conceptualizations that relate to your analyses, and I think it would greatly enrich the contribution of this paper if you were to incorporate them. . . . I suspect it will also enrich your ability to analyze your data if you were to scan related conceptualizations and consider their implications for these data. For example, the discussion of the Sociability act could benefit from the literature on socialization, on first impressions and first encounters (Goffman's work), and on the establishment of rapport (such as the interviewing literature). Similarly, the establishment of master in the Mastery act may be related to the establishment of professionalism or of proficiency. . . . Parents' and clients' cooperation with the Celebratory acts (page 25) seems in part to relate to the norm of reciprocity, or to the contagion effect (when other people laugh, it's hard not to laugh). I don't know that anyone has proposed comedy or humor in these contexts, but making the link to a broader literature is important. By adding such richness you greatly broaden the implications of this effort and the extent to which it will be read and used by other researchers.

In addition to the manuscript's positioning with regard to theoretical conversations on emotions, service encounters, and humor and play, this reviewer highlights a number of other literatures that also may bear on the study's findings.

The strength of this multivocality is that data convey the richness and complexity of real-life interactions. The downside, of course, is that these data may resonate with different reviewers in different ways; hence the suggested changes. In light of this multivocality, it is not surprising that reviewers and editors may suggest significant changes or major additions to manuscripts' theoretical positions. During the review process, then, one of our decisions as authors is whether to incorporate reviewers' suggested changes into our stories and, if so, how much.

We get a first glance at the changes in theoretical positioning that manuscripts undergo by looking at how the titles of these manuscripts changed from original submission to final acceptance. With the exception of the article by Jane Dutton and Janet Dukerich (1991), all of the titles changed, indicating a different theoretical focus for the papers.

Author(s)	Title at Submission	Title at Acceptance
Boje (1995)	A Postmodern Analysis of Disney Leadership: The Story of Storytelling Organization Succession From Feudal Bureaucratic to "Tamara-Land" Discourses	Stories of the Storytelling Organization: A Postmodern Analysis of Disney as "Tamara-Land"

Author(s)	Title at Submission	Title at Acceptance
Dutton and Dukerich (1991)	Keeping an Eye on the Mirror: Image and Identity in Organizational Adaptation	Keeping an Eye on the Mirror: Image and Identity in Organizational Adaptation
Gephart (1993)	Public Inquiry as Performance Occasion: Tracking the Myth of Organization	The Textual Approach: Risk and Blame in Disaster Sensemaking
Golden-Biddle and Rao (in press)	Monitoring as Ritual: A Study of Faith and Facework in Non-Profit Boards	Breaches in the Boardroom: Organizational Identity and Conflicts of Commitment in a Non-Profit Organization
Hatch (in press)	Reading Irony in the Humor of a Management Team: Organizational Contradictions in Context	Irony and the Social Construction of Contradiction in the Humor of a Management Team
Locke (1996a)	Emotion Management in Professional Relationships: A Study of Comedic Microperformances	A Funny Thing Happened: The Management of Consumer Emotions in Service Encounters
Sutton (1991)	Getting the Money: Bill Collectors' Expressed Emotions as Tools of Social Influence Over Debtors	Maintaining Norms About Expressed Emotions: The Case of Bill Collectors

Rewriting the Study's Positioning
in the Extant Literature

Now let us consider the more specific ways in which the articles were rewritten. Our reading of the successive drafts of the manuscripts and the associated reviewer and editor comments indicates that the manuscripts change in their construction of the extant literature. The changes may be relatively minor, for example, when the reviewers suggest that the authors have constructed intertextual fields that need further specification. Or, the changes can be quite marked, for example, when the reviewers and editors suggest that the articles should be positioned in a different intertextual field. In the latter case, in effect they assert that the authors should attempt to join different or additional conversations.

Filling in the Conversation

An example of the first case, in which reviewers make suggestions to complete the intertextual field, is provided by Mary Jo Hatch's (in press) manuscript review process. Following are the reviewer's comments and the paragraph that the author created to respond to that reviewer's request to incorporate additional existing work on related topics. We provide here the author's revised introduction that addressed the reviewer's comments. In addition, the author further addressed these comments at another point later on in the same manuscript revision.

Reviewer Comments	*Author's Manuscript Revision*
I would like to see the author distinguish among concepts in this area. For example, a general paragraph is needed on pp. 3-4 to point out the differences among related constructs in the organizational literature— e.g., paradox, irony, and contradiction. The author acknowledges studies with a similar slant on p. 1 of the paper but tends to drop these studies during the analysis and the interpretation when, in fact, Poole & Van deVen, Quinn & Cameron, and Heydebrand find some related interpretations about transformation that this study reports. Two other articles that are relevant for this study should be cited: Filby & Wilmott . . . and Putnam, L. L.	Several organization researchers adopt an interpretive, constructivist perspective in their studies of organizational contradiction. For example, Ford and Backoff (1988) make a strong case for locating organizational contradiction in the constructions of organizational members but make their argument in relation to paradox rather than contradiction. Benson (1977) and Putnam (1985) both consider contradiction as a way of acknowledging incongruent relations within the constructed social order of organizations, but neither considers the making of contradictory statements as part of the social construction process itself. Most relevant to the study reported here, Filby and Wilmott (1988) describe contradictions in a social service organization as socially constructed. Their work indicates the importance of humor in their interpretation of the contradictions in their case rests heavily on a photocopied cartoon posted throughout the department and on the interpretations department members gave to this cultural artifact.

Similarly, one of Sutton's (1991) reviewers suggested that his manuscript might include a fuller treatment of emotion theory to more clearly identify the work's relevance to that theoretical conversation. In particular, this reviewer commented,

> The paper is well referenced, especially within the psychological literature (maybe too much there, even), and aware of most of the empirical studies I would suggest. There may be more, however, on emotion theory that the author might want to include or return to in the conclusion. This would strengthen the theoretical contribution of the conclusion.

Joining a Different Conversation

In this type of change, the reviewers and/or editors suggest that the studies should be positioned in a different intertextual field. That is, they pose different "theoretical hooks" or conversations for the studies to join. We see this in the case of Karen Golden-Biddle and Huggy Rao's (in press) paper. Specifically, a reviewer questioned one of the conversations the paper originally sought to join, institutional theory, and proposed instead that the conversation on impression management might be more appropriate. These comments are excerpted in the following:

> This is a well-written paper that shows clear understanding of institutional theory. The paper is ambitious in seeking to provide thick descriptions of the relations between directors and top managers and thus clarify

principal/agent relations. The paper also seeks to provide insight on the impression management of conflict events.

Perhaps because of the ambitious nature of the project, the contribution to any one of the above mentioned literatures is not always clear. For example, at the end of the paper, I still wasn't clear whether, in the authors' view, the data supported the view of boards as "pliant pawns or vigilant monitors" (p. 4). How does this study relate back to the agency theory literature that frames the opening of the paper? . . . Then later . . . the institutional framing of the paper seems inappropriate. . . . A more promising perspective is impression management, and here the conjunction of agency theory with impression management mentioned in the discussion is a potential contribution.

The authors did revise their manuscript to incorporate impression management. These changes are developed in the following excerpt, which details the difference between the original and accepted versions of the introduction.

Original Submission	*Accepted Submission*
Considerable debate centers around the nature of the relationship between boards of directors and top managers. Some researchers portray the outside directors *as independent and impartial agents* and contend that outsider-dominated boards are more likely to curtail entrenchment by managers than insider-controlled boards (Fama and	Agency theory, the dominant approach to research on corporate governance, holds that the separation of ownership from management constitutes an efficient division of labor but also recognizes that self-interested top managers, by virtue of their expertise and superior access to information, can misrepresent performance, misallocate resources, and engage in self-dealing at the expense of

Original Submission	*Accepted Submission*
Jensen, 1983). . . . By contrast, other researchers suggest that outsiders are *dependent agents* prone to serving the interests of long serving CEOs in for-profit organizations (Herman, 1981; Hill and Phan, 1991; Davis, 1991) and nonprofit organizations (Herman and Heimovics, 1990). . . . Further insight into this dichotomous portrait of boards as either pliant pawns or vigilant monitors has been impeded by the lack of intensive research on *how* directors monitor top managers and *how* managers relate to their monitors (Middleton, 1987; Stone and Crittenden, 1983). (emphases in original)	shareholders. . . . Organizational sociologists have critiqued the agency theoretic model of boards as limited. . . . (DiMaggio and Zukin, 1991; Granovetter, 1985; Hirsch, Michaels, and Friedman, 1987). . . . There is no empirical work on how the functioning of boards is influenced by the cultural context. Drawing on the social constructionist perspective (cf. Berger and Luckman, 1966; Knorr-Cetina, 1981; Rabinow and Sullivan, 1979), we conceptualize the board role differently than in agency theory. Rather than being an objective entity comprised primarily of fiduciary and legal considerations, we see the board role as constitutive of and inseparable from the shared meanings held by organizational members. . . . Organizational identity—the shared beliefs of members about the central, enduring, and distinctive characteristics of the organization—constitutes part of the shared meanings held by members (Albert and Whetten, 1985; Ashforth and Mael, 1989; Dutton and Dukerich, 1991; Dutton, Dukerich, and Harquail, 1994). . . . Latent

Original Submission	Accepted Submission
	contradictions embedded in perceived organizational identity could be precipitated and become visible during breaches. . . . When faced with such contradictions . . . actors experience role strain (Goode, 1960), which they seek to alleviate by engaging in "facework" (Goffman, 1959, 1967:12).

A similar move is made on the part of reviewers with regard to Jane Dutton and Janet Dukerich's (1991) manuscript. This reviewer acknowledges the location of the paper in the literature on adaptation but sees an additional theoretical conversation for the paper to join. In this case, however, the authors choose not to incorporate the reviewer's suggestion and explain why in their response. In the following, we excerpt both the reviewer's comments and the authors' response to the reviewer:

Reviewer's Comment	Authors' Response to Reviewer
I see that your paper ties into adaptation as the central theoretical thrust of the paper. However, clearly learning is also a broad theoretical issue which is implicitly addressed by your data. I think that you have really under-exploited the possibilities of your data for linkages to learning. You probably don't have the space	We are very limited in our ability to do this given the space limitations and the additional text that we have added in the image and identity sections. We hope that you will find that the revised discussion and implications section does a better job of addressing the question of "So what is new

Reviewer's Comment	Authors' Response to Reviewer
to address this topic. But, if you can, you should, or write your follow[-up] on paper. It's a great opportunity.	here?," particularly in relation to what has been done in the adaptation literature. We decided after some debate that we really did not have room to link explicitly to the learning literature.

Here, the authors' response indicated that, primarily due to space limitations, they could not exploit their study's implications for the conversation on organizational learning, and thus they chose to decline the invitation to write this literature into their study.

The examples we have furnished in this section indicate that although authors have and present their understandings of the theoretical locations relevant for their studies, their reviewer audiences bring their own apprehensions of the literature as well as their own ideas as to relevant conversations for the works to join. Thus the intertextual fields that the broader audience of organizational scholars read in the published works are constructed and reconstructed in the interactions between gatekeepers and authors. The final construction of the intertextual field is a negotiated outcome concerning what constitutes relevant locations for the works. Through this process, the reviewers do participate in rewriting the positioning of our studies.

Tightening the Theory-Data Coupling

Reviewers also requested that the relationship between the theoretical points or proposed storylines and the contextual evidence be rewritten to tighten the coupling between the two in the theorized story. Specifically, they wanted tighter linkages established between theoretical insight and evidence from the field. As our discussion of telling and showing in Chapter 3 indicated, the reviewers focus both on differentiating data from interpretation and, at the same time, on tightly coupling them. Reviewers want to both see the data (i.e., showing) and understand its significance (i.e., telling). So, a reviewer on Mary Jo Hatch's (in press) paper, for example, asked,

> In the instance that you examine, how does ironic humor serve contradictory purposes of stabilizing experience while changing it? Go back to your text to illustrate how these claims operate in your data.

Similarly, the consulting editor on Jane Dutton and Janet Dukerich's (1991) article maintained,

> The authors need to bolster the evidence presented that the [Port Authority]'s responses follow from that identity or are a reflection of that identity. This could be attacked in a number of ways including elaborating contrasting cases (different identity, different responses) or alternative responses available to the [Port Authority] (or perhaps even considered by it) which were not selected. Knowing your data better than your reviewers, there are perhaps a number of ways in which you could approach this. However, the link does need to be strengthened.

Both of these comments indicate a concern with the relationship between theoretical points and data as they are written into the articles. In the case of Mary Jo Hatch, the reviewer directs that her theorizing be expressed through her excerpts of managers' conversations. In the case of Jane Dutton and Janet Dukerich, the consulting editor directs the authors to write additional data into their manuscript to shore up the claim that the actions the Port Authority took stemmed from its concern with maintaining its identity.

At the same time as the review process underscores the need to write together interpretation and evidence—telling and showing—it emphasizes the need to maintain the distinction between these two elements. These editor comments, also from the "Eye on the Mirror" article (Dutton & Dukerich, 1991), illustrate this concern:

> It is sometimes difficult to distinguish the authors' interpretation from actual data provided by your informants. Your second reviewer raises several questions of this nature. Please review the manuscript to clarify the source: "the stain on that beauty" comment is an interesting one, but the reader needs to know to whom to attribute it.

Simplifying the Storyline

Occasionally, the review process calls for more significant rewritings of the theorized stories. In particular, authors sometimes were asked to select out some aspects of their data and claims in favor of a single most interesting development. This is perhaps an anomaly of writing for the genre of journals, where space constraints loom larger than they do in books.

The following reviewer comments addressed to Karen Golden-Biddle and Huggy Rao (in press) illustrate an enjoinder to selectively rewrite the theorized story:

It is my judgment that the findings are stated too broadly and too generally. The paper needs more focus and the data need to be organized in a more compelling way around this focus. . . . Currently your work supports a lot of ideas that are fairly well known (and thus the data illustrate another application of these ideas), as well as introducing other ideas that are less well understood, provocative, and I think important. I'll try to isolate what I see as claims falling into each of these categories. In doing this, my hope is that you can adjust the focus of the paper and the discussion of your research to highlight claims which fit the latter category. I think this is where your work adds really important insights. I would like you to more fully develop these insights, make the core claims more noticeable and understandable by using more data that are more varied in kind.

These comments point to two underlying assumptions about the stories we can tell in our journal articles. Not surprisingly, the first is that the theorized stories need to be unique. Consistent with the view that the review process helps to determine the potential contribution of a study, this reviewer underscores the need to write into a central position in the manuscript the portions of the theorized story that offer less well-understood, provocative ideas. The more familiar ideas, then, should be erased. Second, the points we make should be concise; given the space limitations imposed by journals, we are able to write only one theorized story.

Similarly, the following comments by Bob Sutton's (1991) editor emphasize this selection process and, at the same time, further bring home the second assumption:

A most severely limiting feature is that the exact contribution being pursued with these observations is not clearly articulated for the reader and perhaps not clear for the author. Especially unclear is the purpose being pursued for an audience of organizational scientists. The paper appears to be pursuing several goals at once: (1) a description of the functioning of a credit card collection organization; (2) a theory of motivation for debt repayment; (3) a set of your own and your respondents' theories about the impact of collectors' tactics in influencing debtors; (4) a theory about how collectors control their personal emotions to maintain control in a conversation with debtors. All but the first of these has little to do with organizations per se. . . . Regardless, there appears to be too many goals being pursued within the confines of a single study. Thus, as a first recommendation towards revision, we recommend that you try to focus your project to a more singular and coherent objective relevant to organizational social science. . . . You can of course pursue any of these themes. But a single short paper cannot hold up to the burden of pursuing them all simultaneously. Thus we recommend that you take a firm choice about one of these themes and forget the others for the sake of this presentation.

Refocusing the Storyline

Sometimes the process of selecting out certain parts of the story results in a quite different focus for the manuscripts than does the one originally presented by authors. In Bob Sutton's (1991) original submission, for example, the focus is on the expression of emotion as a way in which to bring about a certain kind of compliance behavior: paying debts. The final version, however, is concerned with the ways in which organizations attempt to preserve their "rules" for emotional expression. Because the agent in the story changes from emotions to organizations, the paper changes from presenting a theory about emotional influence to presenting a theory about organizational control. These differences are clearly reflected in the different titles of the paper presented earlier, and they are outlined in the abstracts of the original and final versions of this paper, as presented in the following:

Original Submission of Abstract	Final Version of Abstract

This paper proposes a middle-range theory of the expression of emotion by bill collectors to debtors, grounded in a qualitative study at a collection organization. . . . Collectors use a negative reinforcement scheme to garner payments: They induce anxiety with a relentless stream of warnings that most debtors can escape only by paying their bills. Collectors typically begin conversations with an "urgent" tone (high arousal with a hint of disapproval) to amplify debtor anxiety about factual warnings. If debtors don't sound sufficiently upset, then collectors routinely express stronger negative emotions to provoke anxiety. Conversely, collectors try to convey calmness to angry debtors to avoid a cycle of escalating hostility. These contingencies cause
A qualitative study of a bill collection organization was used to identify norms about the emotions that collectors are expected to convey to debtors and the means used by the organization to maintain such norms given that collectors' expressed emotions are simultaneously influenced by their inner feelings. These data indicate that collectors are selected, socialized, and rewarded for following the general norm of conveying urgency (high arousal with a hint of irritation) to debtors. Collectors are further socialized and rewarded to adjust their expressed emotions in response to variations in debtor demeanor. These contingent norms sometimes clash with collectors' feelings towards debtors.

Original Submission of Abstract	Final Version of Abstract
emotive dissonance when expressed emotions best for wielding influence clash with collectors' inner feelings. Collectors sometimes express emotions that reduce compliance, especially anger. Typically, however, they use coping strategies to avoid becoming angry or to release anger without communicating it to debtors. The discussion focuses on implications for theory about expressed emotions as tools of influence in organizations.	Bill collectors are taught to cope with such emotive dissonance by using cognitive appraisals that help them become emotionally detached from debtors and by releasing unpleasant feelings without communicating these emotions to debtors. The discussion focuses on the implications of this research for developing general theory about the expression of emotion in organizational life.

Similarly, in the case of David Boje's (1995) article, the theorized story changed from a quantitative and qualitative analysis of the storytelling styles and performances of Disney's three chief executive officers (CEOs) to a theorized, discursive analysis of storytelling and its critical implications for the expression of marginal voices in organizations and in organizational studies.

Original Submission of Abstract	Final Version of Abstract
This paper is an analysis of storytelling behavior of three CEOs of the Walt Disney Corporation. Disney is conceptualized as a historical succession of storytelling organizations that have adapted	My purpose is to theorize Walt Disney enterprises as a storytelling organization in which an active-reactive interplay of premodern, modern, and postmodern discourses occurs.

Original Submission of Abstract	*Final Version of Abstract*
over time in concert with leader succession. The analysis is done in three parts: 1) the mechanics of leaders' storytelling style differences, 2) a deconstruction of stories and storytelling performances of the three CEOs, 3) the succession of storytelling organizations from feudal to bureaucratic to "Tamara." The major contribution of the paper is to illustrate differences in the storytelling performances and succession storytelling organizations and to deconstruct some of the storytelling culture at Disney.	A postmodern analysis of these multiple discourses reveals the marginalized voices and excluded stories of a darker side of the Disney legend. *Tamara,* a play that is also a discursive metaphor, is used to demonstrate a plurivocal (multiple story interpretation) theory of competing organizational discourses. Subsequent sections address storytelling, organizational theory, analyses of official accounts of Disney enterprises, and less well-known, even contrary accounts. The article concludes with implications for postmodern theory and future storytelling research projects.

In "The Textual Approach: Risk and Blame in Disaster Sensemaking," Bob Gephart (1993) intended to theorize our notions of managerial control and organization as fragile and illusory through the story of the natural gas liquids explosion that resulted in the deaths of two men. However, as part of a special issue forum that was intended to highlight configural approaches to organization, the review process identified the methods by which the story was disclosed as most interesting. When the theorized story was rewritten, it focused on the use of the textual approach in organizational analysis. The story of the disaster was subordinated to the study's methodological story, and the idea that organization itself is a myth disappeared from the manuscript.

What we see, then, from these authors' experiences is that the review process typically involves significant rewriting efforts. That reviewers and editors become differently engaged with our manuscripts points to their relevance and import for the field of organizational studies. It also points out, however, that the particular relevance and import need to be negotiated to greater or lesser degrees. Reviewers' and editors' suggestions for rewriting focus on questions of significance: What is the theoretical significance of the data, and which conversations should the study join? Rewriting our stories, then, takes center stage during the review process.

Concluding Comments

We wrote this book to break the silence on writing and, more generally, to demystify the process of writing. By placing writing matters center stage, we hope that we have provided you, our readers, with both thought-provoking and practical avenues for becoming more reflexive and knowledgeable about writing. Through dialogue on writing, we believe, we only further strengthen our scientific efforts; we generate enthusiasm and curiosity for developing theoretical points about organizations, render these points more accessible to a wider variety of audiences, and ultimately gain greater insight about the organizations and organization members we experience as well as about ourselves.

Through our experiences of writing, our conversations about writing, and the process of writing this book, we have come to believe that the most insightful and compelling stories are those that tackle issues that matter to the authors and readers as well as to the people in the field. Our stories are about basic and compelling human situations faced by organization members whose everyday lives we experienced. And they also are about basic human commitments in science, for when we strip away and demystify the overtly scientific discussion of appropriate method and explanation, we see our struggles with deciding which philosophical ideas to hold, how to apprehend and represent the human reality we investigate, and so on. It is on these most fundamental human conversations in science that our contributions—our theoretical points—are constructed.

What does it mean, from a writing perspective, for stories to deal with issues that matter? We offer four preliminary thoughts on this question. First, stories that we write in journal articles must embody at least a theoretical complication with illustrative field-based data. That is, they must pose a problem in the existing theoretical conversation that is significant to the community of readers. This problem piques reader curiosity on how it will be resolved and, perhaps more important, piques reader curiosity on the implications of the resolution for the theoretical conversation. Readers wonder how this conversation will change as a result of the study. Additionally, these theoretical complications need to be, at a minimum, coupled with field data that provide illustrative examples.

However, and to our second point, the better stories do more than incorporate field data as illustrations. They actually embody a field-based complication. That is, members of the organization face a problem, dilemma, or paradox that, in its own right, is significant to them. It matters deeply to them, and they struggle diligently to resolve it. Moreover, this problem gives us insight into our theoretical complication. Although a nested story in our articles, it is not merely illustrative; it becomes central and figural. Thus the theoretical and field complications (i.e., both the local and more general experiences and problems) become mutually interdependent, each informing, enriching, and shaping the other.

Third, the stories have resolutions, and these resolutions address the identified problems. A resolution for the theoretical story addresses the specific problem identified in the extant theoretical conversation, whereas a resolution for the field-base story concerns how members dealt with their problematic situation. Moreover, these problems must have solutions, that is, resolutions to the complications. This is no small feat given that we face a variety of problematic situations in the field (as well as in life in general), most of which do not have endings or which take a long time for a resolution to be reached. Furthermore, the resolution must fit the complication. Unless the complication is resolved and the complication and resolution cohere, it is useless as a story; it provides no insight into how humans deal successfully with troublesome situations. The better stories illuminate new or unique ways in which to handle problems and often provide significant insights by portraying successful resolutions of problems.

Finally, the better stories inform and teach in a way that the readers learn in the reading. Readers, bringing their own experiences to the reading, are able to converse with the articles. The stories resonate with the readers, perhaps challenging and provoking them into considering alternative per-

articles. The stories resonate with the readers, perhaps challenging and provoking them into considering alternative perspectives, ideas, and ways of viewing organizational phenomena.

At the point of bringing this book to a close, we are 7 years into our exploration of writing matters in our profession—with, we might add, no end yet in sight! We now think about the writing moment (Van Maanen, 1995) in our knowledge-creating efforts quite differently, appreciating much more the complexity of the task we are setting out to accomplish when we sit down to our keyboards, or pencil and paper, to write. In Chapter 1, we played off the "just write it up" injunction to outline this complexity. By doing this, we highlighted a misperception of writing as the residual task in our research efforts. Certainly, writing is not residual! Mary Jo Hatch, one of the authors whose article was used as an illustration, put it very well when she reflected that perhaps we should draw our boundaries around the research process more widely. Instead of assuming that an investigative effort has achieved closure when the analysis is complete and insights have been formulated, we should extend our definition of research to include the drafting of a formal paper, revision efforts during the review process, and the readings the work receives from our community of scientists. In this view, writing is one of several research processes with which we need to develop increasing competency. In addition, we have to develop our own processes for writing. We offer writing and rewriting, sharing, and reading as what we hope are some helpful ways in which to continue to think about writing matters and to develop our own writing processes.

Writing and Rewriting

Experienced writers testify that good writing demands investments of time and effort in a recursive writing process (Elbow, 1981; Fulweiler, 1987). Certainly, the organization stories that our data-gathering and analytic efforts authorize us to write precede the main writing stage of our work. Yet, in a very real sense, these stories also grow out of the writing process. Only by getting our points down on paper can we make them available for closer examination. When we and others interact with our words, we inevitably modify and rewrite what we are trying to say. We have to iteratively rewrite our way to writing that displays orderliness, coherence, and a conscious strategy for theorizing our experiences in the field. Knowing this makes us more patient with each draft.

Sharing

We think it is important to share from the very beginning both what we write about and our experiences of writing. As we write successive drafts, we need readers to tell us how they experience our words (Elbow, 1981), how they understand the theoretical stories we are trying to tell, and what significance they see for the work. Jane Dutton underscored how generous people were in offering their responses to drafts of the "Eye on the Mirror" manuscript (Dutton & Dukerich, 1991), indicating the potential for contribution that they saw in that work. She emphasized that these readers could see why the work was interesting in ways that neither she nor Janet Dukerich, her coauthor, could articulate. Similarly, sharing experiences of the writing process helps to break the silence we referred to in our introduction and creates support for this lengthy process. This suggests that we should make writing a social process from the beginning, creating our own informal network of readers who will respond to our writing before it is submitted for review.

Reading

Finally, we have found the process of reading manuscripts with an eye toward how they are written to be invaluable. As this book indicates, reading in this manner not only helps to demystify the writing process but, by helping us to become aware of the variety of writing evident in journal manuscripts, also helps us to develop our own writing styles and voices. By looking at variations in written presentations and styles, we find that we more closely identify with the work of some authors while finding that we perhaps do not want to emulate others (Locke & Brazelton, in press). This helps us to identify over time what we want to sound like on paper.

As we close this book, we look forward to continuing conversations about writing matters with you.

Appendix

Articles Used as Illustrations

Adler, P. A., & Adler, P. (1988). Intense loyalty in organizations: A case study of college athletics. *Administrative Science Quarterly, 33,* 401-417.

Barley, S. R. (1983). Semiotics and the study of occupational and organizational cultures. *Administrative Science Quarterly, 28,* 393-413.

Barley, S. R., & Kunda, G. (1992). Design and devotion: Surges of rational and normative ideologies of control in managerial discourse. *Administrative Science Quarterly, 37,* 363-399.

Bartunek, J. M. (1984). Changing interpretive schemes and organizational restructuring: The example of a religious order. *Administrative Science Quarterly, 9,* 355-372.

Biggart, N. W., & Hamilton, G. G. (1984). The power of obedience. *Administrative Science Quarterly, 29,* 540-549.

Bills, D. B. (1987). Costs, commitment, and rewards: Factors influencing the design and implementation of internal labor markets. *Administrative Science Quarterly, 32,* 202-221.

Boje, D. M. (1991). The storytelling organization: A study of story performance in an office-supply firm. *Administrative Science Quarterly, 36,* 106-126.

Boje, D. M. (1995). Stories of the storytelling organization: A postmodern analysis of Disney as "Tamara-Land." *Academy of Management Journal, 38,* 997-1035.

Dutton, J. E., & Dukerich, J. M. (1991). Keeping an eye on the mirror: Image and identity in organizational adaptation. *Academy of Management Journal, 34,* 517-554.

Eisenhardt, K. M. (1989). Making fast strategic decisions in high-velocity environments. *Academy of Management Journal, 32,* 543-576.

Elsbach, K. D., & Sutton, R. I. (1992). Acquiring organizational legitimacy through illegitimate actions: A marriage of institutional and impression management theories. *Academy of Management Journal, 35,* 699-738.

Gephart, R. P. (1993). The textual approach: Risk and blame in disaster sensemaking. *Academy of Management Journal, 36,* 1465-1514.

Gersick, C.J.G. (1988). Time and transition in work teams: Toward a new model of group development. *Academy of Management Journal, 31,* 9-41.

Gersick, C.J.G. (1994). Pacing strategic change: The case of a new venture. *Academy of Management Journal, 37,* 9-45.

Golden-Biddle, K., & Rao, H. V. (in press). Breaches in the boardroom: Organizational identity and conflicts of commitment in a non-profit organization. *Organization Science.*

Gronn, P. G. (1983). Talk as the work: The accomplishment of school administration. *Administrative Science Quarterly, 28,* 1-21.

Hatch, M. J. (in press). Irony and the social construction of contradiction in the humor of a management team. *Organization Science.*

Hirschhorn, L., & Gilmore, T. (1980). The application of family therapy concepts to influencing organizational behavior. *Administrative Science Quarterly, 25,* 18-37.

Holm, P. ((1995). The dynamics of institutionalization: Transformation processes in Norwegian fisheries. *Administrative Science Quarterly, 40,* 398-422.

Isabella, L. A. (1990). Evolving interpretations as a change unfolds: How managers construe key organizational events. *Academy of Management Journal, 33,* 7-41.

Kahn, W. A. (1993). Caring for the caregivers: Patterns of organizational caregiving. *Administrative Science Quarterly, 38,* 539-563.

Kram, K. E. (1983). Phases of the mentor relationship. *Academy of Management Journal, 26,* 608-625.

Kram, K. E., & Isabella, L. A. (1985). Mentoring alternatives: The role of peer relationships in career development. *Academy of Management Journal, 28,* 110-132.

Lammers, C. J. (1988). The interorganizational control of an occupied country. *Administrative Science Quarterly, 33,* 438-457.

Langton, J. (1984). The ecological theory of bureaucracy: The case of Josiah Wedgwood and the British pottery industry. *Administrative Science Quarterly, 29,* 330-354.

Locke, K. D. (1996a). A funny thing happened: The management of consumer emotions in service encounters. *Organization Science, 7,* 40-59.

EDITOR'S NOTE: Breaches in the boardroom: Organization at identity and conflicts of commitment in a nonprofit organization, K. Golden-Biddle & H. V. Rao, *Organization Science* (1993), The Institute of Management Sciences (INFORMS), 2 Charles Street, Suite 300, Providence, RI 02904, reprinted by permission.

Meyerson, D. E. (1994). Interpretations of stress in institutions: The cultural production of ambiguity and burnout. *Administrative Science Quarterly, 39,* 628-653.

Pentland, B. T. (1992). Organizing moves in software support hotlines. *Administrative Science Quarterly, 37,* 527-548.

Prasad, P. (1993). Symbolic processes in the implementation of technological change: A symbolic interactionist study of work computerization. *Academy of Management Journal, 36,* 1400-1429.

Rafaeli, A. (1989). When cashiers meet customers: An analysis of the role of supermarket cashiers. *Academy of Management Journal, 32,* 245-273.

Rafaeli, A., & Sutton, R. I. (1991). Emotional contrast strategies as means of social influence: Lessons from criminal interrogators and bill collectors. *Academy of Management Journal, 34,* 749-775.

Riley, P. (1983). A structurationist account of political culture. *Administrative Science Quarterly, 28,* 414-437.

Ross, J., & Staw, B. M. (1993). Organizational escalation and exit: Lessons from the Shoreham nuclear power plant. *Academy of Management Journal, 36,* 701-732.

Skoldberg, K. (1994). Tales of change: Public administration reform and narrative mode. *Organization Science, 5,* 219-238.

Sutton, R. I. (1987). The process of organizational death: Disbanding and reconnecting. *Administrative Science Quarterly, 32,* 542-569.

Sutton, R. I. (1991). Maintaining norms about expressed emotions: The case of bill collectors. *Administrative Science Quarterly, 36,* 245-268.

Sutton, R. I., & Callahan, A. (1987). The stigma of bankruptcy: Spoiled organizational image and its management. *Academy of Management Journal, 30,* 405-436.

Thomas, D. A. (1993). Racial dynamics in cross-race developmental relationships. *Administrative Science Quarterly, 38,* 169-194.

Turner, B. A. (1976). The organizational and interorganizational development of disasters. *Administrative Science Quarterly, 21,* 378-397.

Vaughan, D. (1990). Autonomy, interdependence, and social control: NASA and the space shuttle *Challenger. Administrative Science Quarterly, 35,* 225-257.

Weick, K. E. (1993). The collapse of sensemaking in organizations: The Mann Gulch disaster. *Administrative Science Quarterly, 38,* 628-652.

Yan, A., & Gray, B. (1994). Bargaining power: Management control and performance in United States-China joint ventures—A comparative case study. *Academy of Management Journal, 37,* 1478-1717.

EDITOR'S NOTE: The organizational and interorganizational development of disasters, B. A. Turner, published in *Administrative Science Quarterly* Vol. 21, No. 3. (September 1976), reprinted by permission of *Administrative Science Quarterly.*

References

Adler, P. A., & Adler, P. (1988). Intense loyalty in organizations: A case study of college athletics. *Administrative Science Quarterly, 33,* 401-417.

Aronson, N. (1984). Science as a claims making activity: Implications for social problems research. In J. W. Schneider & J. Kitsuse (Eds.), *Studies in the sociology of social problems* (pp. 1-30). Norwood, NJ: Ablex.

Atkinson, P. (1990). *The ethnographic imagination.* London: Rutledge.

Barley, S. R. (1983). Semiotics and the study of occupational and organizational cultures. *Administrative Science Quarterly, 28,* 393-413.

Barley, S. R., & Kunda, G. (1992). Design and devotion: Surges of rational and normative ideologies of control in managerial discourse. *Administrative Science Quarterly, 37,* 363-399.

Bartunek, J. M. (1984). Changing interpretive schemes and organizational restructuring: The example of a religious order. *Administrative Science Quarterly, 9,* 355-372.

Bazerman, C. (1993). Intertextual self-fashioning: Gould and Lewontin's representations of the literature. In J. Selzer (Ed.), *Understanding scientific prose* (pp. 20-41). Madison: University of Wisconsin Press.

Bazerman, C., & Paradis, J. (1991). *Textual dynamics of the professions: Historical and contemporary studies of writing in professional communities.* Madison: University of Wisconsin Press.

Becker, H. (1986). *Writing for social scientists*. Chicago: University of Chicago Press.

Beyer, J. M., Chanove, R. G., & Fox, W. B. (1995). The review process and the facts of manuscripts submitted to *AMJ. Academy of Management Journal, 38,* 1219-1260.

Biggart, N. W., & Hamilton, G. G. (1984). The power of obedience. *Administrative Science Quarterly, 29,* 540-549.

Billig, M. (1993). Psychology, rhetoric, and cognition. In R. H. Roberts and J. M. Good (Eds.), *The recovery of rhetoric: Persuasive discourse and disciplinarity in the human sciences* (pp. 119-136). Charlottesville: University Press of Virginia.

Bills, D. B. (1987). Costs, commitment, and rewards: Factors influencing the design and implementation of internal labor markets. *Administrative Science Quarterly, 32,* 202-221.

Boje, D. M. (1991). The storytelling organization: A study of story performance in an office-supply firm. *Administrative Science Quarterly, 36,* 106-126.

Boje, D. M. (1995). Stories of the storytelling organization: A postmodern analysis of Disney as "Tamara-Land." *Academy of Management Journal, 38,* 997-1035.

Booth, W. C. (1961). *The rhetoric of fiction*. Chicago: University of Chicago Press.

Booth, W. C. (1967). The revival of rhetorics. In M. Steinmann, Jr. (Ed.), *New rhetorics* (pp. 1-15). New York: Scribner.

Brooks, C., & Warren, R. P. (1938). *Understanding poetry*. New York: Holt, Rinehart & Winston.

Burke, K. (1950). *A rhetoric of motives*. Berkeley: University of California Press.

Calas, M., & Smircich, L. (1991). Voicing seduction to silence leadership. *Organization Studies, 12,* 567-602.

Campbell, D. T. (1975). Degrees of freedom and the case study. *Comparative Political Studies, 8,* 178-193.

Clifford, J. (1983). On ethnographic authority. *Representations, 1,* 118-146.

Cozzens, S. (1985). Comparing the sciences: Citation context analysis of papers from neuropharmacology and the sociology of science. *Social Studies of Science, 15,* 127-153.

Dutton, J. E., & Dukerich, J. M. (1991). Keeping an eye on the mirror: Image and identity in organizational adaptation. *Academy of Management Journal, 34,* 517-554.

Edmonson, R. (1984). *Rhetoric in sociology*. London: Macmillan.

Eisenhardt, K. M. (1989). Making fast strategic decisions in high-velocity environments. *Academy of Management Journal, 32,* 543-576.

Elbow, P. (1981). *Writing with power: Techniques for mastering the writing process*. New York: Oxford University Press.

Elsbach, K. D., & Sutton, R. I. (1992). Acquiring organizational legitimacy through illegitimate actions: A marriage of institutional and impression management theories. *Academy of Management Journal, 35,* 699-738.

Feldman, M. (1995). *Strategies for interpreting qualitative data.* Thousand Oaks, CA: Sage.

Fine, G. A. (1988, Summer). The ten commandments of writing. *The American Sociologist,* pp. 152-157.

Franklin, J. (1994). *Writing for story.* New York: Penguin Books.

Frost, P. J., & Taylor, R. N. (1995). Partisan perspective: A multiple-level interpretation of the manuscript review process in social science journals. In L. L. Cummings & P. J. Frost (Eds.), *Publishing in the organizational sciences* (pp. 4-43). Thousand Oaks, CA: Sage.

Fulweiler, T. (1987). *Teaching with writing.* Upper Montclair, NJ: Boynton/Cook.

Geertz, C. (1973). *The interpretation of cultures.* New York: Basic Books.

Geertz, C. (1988). *Works and lives: The anthropologist as author.* Stanford, CA: Stanford University Press.

Gephart, R. (1986). Deconstructing the defense for quantification in social science: A content analysis of journal articles on the parametric strategy. *Qualitative Sociology, 9,* 126-144.

Gephart, R. (1988). *Ethnostatistics: Qualitative foundations for quantitative research.* Newbury Park, CA: Sage.

Gephart, R. P. (1978). Status degradation and organizational succession: An ethnomethodological approach. *Administrative Science Quarterly, 23,* 553-581.

Gephart, R. P. (1993). The textual approach: Risk and blame in disaster sensemaking. *Academy of Management Journal, 36,* 1465-1514.

Gersick, C.J.G. (1988). Time and transition in work teams: Toward a new model of group development. *Academy of Management Journal, 31,* 9-41.

Gersick, C.J.G. (1994). Pacing strategic change: The case of a new venture. *Academy of Management Journal, 37,* 9-45.

Gilbert, N. (1976). The transformation of research findings into scientific knowledge. *Social Studies of Science, 6,* 281-306.

Gilbert, N. (1977). Referencing as persuasion. *Social Studies of Science, 7,* 113-122.

Glaser, B., & Strauss, A. (1967). *The discovery of grounded theory.* Chicago: Aldine.

Golden, K. A. (1992). The individual and organizational culture: Strategies for action in highly-ordered contexts. *Journal of Management Studies, 29,* 1-22.

Golden-Biddle, K., & Locke, K. (1993). Appealing work: An investigation of how ethnographic texts convince. *Organization Science, 4,* 595-616.

Golden-Biddle, K., & Rao, H. V. (in press). Breaches in the boardroom: Organizational identity and conflicts of commitment in a non-profit organization. *Organization Science.*

Gould, S. J., & Lewontin, R. (1979). The spandrels of San Marco and the Panglossian paradigm: A critique of the adaptationist programme. *Biological Sciences, 205,* 581-598. (Proceedings of the Royal Society of London)

Gronn, P. G. (1983). Talk as the work: The accomplishment of school administration. *Administrative Science Quarterly, 28,* 1-21.

Gusfield, J. (1981). *The culture of public problems: Drinking, driving and symbolic order.* Chicago: University of Chicago Press.

Hamilton, E., & Cairns, H. (1961). *Plato: The collected dialogues.* Princeton, NJ: Princeton University Press.

Hatch, M. J. (in press). Irony and the social construction of contradiction in the humor of a management team. *Organization Science.*

Hirschhorn, L., & Gilmore, T. (1980). The application of family therapy concepts to influencing organizational behavior. *Administrative Science Quarterly, 25,* 18-37.

Holm, P. ((1995). The dynamics of institutionalization: Transformation processes in Norwegian fisheries. *Administrative Science Quarterly, 40,* 398-422.

Hunter, A. (1990). Rhetoric in research: Networks of knowledge. In A. Hunter (Ed.), *The rhetoric of social research: Understood and believed* (pp. 1-22). New Brunswick, NJ: Rutgers University Press.

Isabella, L. A. (1990). Evolving interpretations as a change unfolds: How managers construe key organizational events. *Academy of Management Journal, 33,* 7-41.

Iser, W. (1978). *The act of reading: A theory of aesthetic response.* Baltimore, MD: Johns Hopkins University Press.

Iser, W. (1989). *Prospecting: From reader response to literary anthropology.* Baltimore, MD: Johns Hopkins University Press.

Kahn, W. A. (1993). Caring for the caregivers: Patterns of organizational caregiving. *Administrative Science Quarterly, 38,* 539-563.

Kilduff, M. (1993). Deconstructing organizations. *Academy of Management Review, 18,* 13-31.

Knorr-Cetina, K. (1981). *The manufacture of knowledge: An essay on the constructivist and contextual nature of science.* New York: Pergamon.

Kram, K. E. (1983. Phases of the mentor relationship. *Academy of Management Journal, 26,* 608-625.

Kram, K. E., & Isabella, L. A. (1985). Mentoring alternatives: The role of peer relationships in career development. *Academy of Management Journal, 28,* 110-132.

Lammers, C. J. (1988). The interorganizational control of an occupied country. *Administrative Science Quarterly, 33,* 438-457.

Langer, S. (1964). *Philosophy in a new key: A study in the symbolism of reason, rite, and art.* New York: Mentor Books.

Langton, J. (1984). The ecological theory of bureaucracy: The case of Josiah Wedgwood and the British pottery industry. *Administrative Science Quarterly, 29,* 330-354.

Latour, B. (1987). *Science in action: How to follow scientists and engineers through society.* Cambridge, MA: Harvard University Press.

Latour, B., & Woolgar, S. (1986). *Laboratory life: The construction of scientific facts.* Princeton, NJ: Princeton University Press.

Law, J., & Williams, R. (1982). Putting the facts together: A study of scientific persuasion. *Social Studies of Science, 12,* 535-558.

Locke, K. D. (1996a). A funny thing happened: The management of consumer emotions in service encounters. *Organization Science, 7,* 40-59.

Locke, K. (1996b). Who's re-writing grounded theory over 25 years later? *Journal of Management Inquiry, 5,* 239-245.

Locke, K., & Brazelton, J. (in press). Why do we ask them to write? Or, whose writing is it, anyway? *Journal of Management Education.*

Locke, K., & Golden-Biddle, K. (in press). Constructing opportunities for contribution: Intertextual coherence and problematization in organizational studies. *Academy of Management Journal.*

Lyne, J. (1993). Angels in the architecture: A Burkean inventional perspective on "Spandrels." In J. Selzer (Ed.), *Understanding scientific prose* (pp. 144-158). Madison: University of Wisconsin Press.

Maclean, N. (1992). *Young men and fire.* Chicago: University of Chicago Press.

March, J., & Simon, H. (1958). *Organizations.* New York: John Wiley.

Marcus, G. (1980). Rhetoric and the ethnographic genre in anthropological research. *Current Anthropology, 21,* 507-510.

Marcus, G., & Cushman, D. (1982). Ethnographies as texts. *Annual Review of Anthropology, 11,* 25-69.

Marcus, G., & Fischer, M. (1986). *Anthropology as cultural critique.* Chicago: University of Chicago Press.

McCloskey, D. (1985). *The rhetoric of economics.* Madison: University of Wisconsin Press.

McCloskey, D. (1990). *If you're so smart: The narrative of economic expertise.* Chicago: University of Chicago Press.

McCloskey, D. (1994). *Knowledge and persuasion in economics.* Cambridge, England: Cambridge University Press.

McGill, L. (1990). Doing science by the numbers: The role of tables and other representational conventions in scientific journal articles. In A. Hunter (Ed.), *The rhetoric of social research: Believed and understood* (pp. 129-141). New Brunswick, NJ: Rutgers University Press.

Meyerson, D. E. (1994). Interpretations of stress in institutions: The cultural production of ambiguity and burnout. *Administrative Science Quarterly, 39,* 628-653.

Morner, K., & Rausch, R. (1991). *NTC's dictionary of literary terms.* Chicago: NTC.

Mulkay, M. (1985). *The word and the world: Explorations in the form of sociological analysis.* Boston: Allen and Unwin.

Mumby, D., & Putnam, L. (1992). Bounded rationality and organizing: A feminist critique. *Academy of Management Review, 17,* 465-486.

Pentland, B. T. (1992). Organizing moves in software support hotlines. *Administrative Science Quarterly, 37,* 527-548.

Pinder, C., & Bourgeois, V. W. (1982). Controlling tropes in administrative science. *Administrative Science Quarterly, 27,* 641-652.

Prasad, P. (1993). Symbolic processes in the implementation of technological change: A symbolic interactionist study of work computerization. *Academy of Management Journal, 36,* 1400-1429.

Rafaeli, A. (1989). When cashiers meet customers: An analysis of the role of supermarket cashiers. *Academy of Management Journal, 32,* 245-273.

Rafaeli, A., & Sutton, R. I. (1991). Emotional contrast strategies as means of social influence: Lessons from criminal interrogators and bill collectors. *Academy of Management Journal, 34,* 749-775.

Richardson, L. (1994). Writing: A method of inquiry. In N. K. Denzin & Y. S. Lincoln (Eds.), *Handbook of qualitative research* (pp. 516-529). Thousand Oaks, CA: Sage.

Riley, P. (1983). A structurationist account of political culture. *Administrative Science Quarterly, 28,* 414-437.

Rorty, R. (1967). *The linguistic turn: Recent essays in philosophical method.* Chicago: University of Chicago Press.

Rorty, R. (1982). *The consequences of pragmatism.* Minneapolis: University of Minnesota Press.

Ross, J., & Staw, B. M. (1993). Organizational escalation and exit: Lessons from the Shoreham nuclear power plant. *Academy of Management Journal, 36,* 701-732.

Rousseau, D. (1995). Publishing from a reviewer's perspective. In L. L. Cummings and P. J. Frost (Eds.), *Publishing in the organizational sciences* (pp. 151-163). Thousand Oaks, CA: Sage.

Selzer, J. (1993). *Understanding scientific prose.* Madison: University of Wisconsin Press.

Skoldberg, K. (1994). Tales of change: Public administration reform and narrative mode. *Organization Science, 5,* 219-238.

Spector, M., & Kitsuse, J. I. (1977). *Constructing social problems.* Redwood City, CA: Benjamin Cummings.

Strauss, A. L. (1987). *Qualitative analysis for social scientists.* Cambridge, England: Cambridge University Press.

Strauss, A. L., & Corbin, J. (1990). *Basics of qualitative research: Grounded theory procedures and techniques.* Newbury Park, CA: Sage.

Sutton, R. I. (1987). The process of organizational death: Disbanding and reconnecting. *Administrative Science Quarterly, 32,* 542-569.

Sutton, R. I. (1991). Maintaining norms about expressed emotions: The case of bill collectors. *Administrative Science Quarterly, 36,* 245-268.

Sutton, R. I., & Callahan, A. (1987). The stigma of bankruptcy: Spoiled organizational image and its management. *Academy of Management Journal, 30,* 405-436.

Thomas, D. A. (1993). Racial dynamics in cross-race developmental relationships. *Administrative Science Quarterly, 38,* 169-194.

Turner, B. A. (1976). The organizational and interorganizational development of disasters. *Administrative Science Quarterly, 21,* 378-397.

Van Maanen, J. (1988). *Tales of the field: On writing ethnography.* Chicago: University of Chicago Press.

Van Maanen, J. (1995). *Representation in ethnography.* Thousand Oaks, CA: Sage.

Vaughan, D. (1990). Autonomy, interdependence, and social control: NASA and the space shuttle *Challenger. Administrative Science Quarterly, 35,* 225-257.

Watson, T. J. (1995). Shaping the story: Rhetoric, persuasion, and creative writing in organizational ethnography. *Studies in Cultures, Organizations and Societies, 1,* 301-311.

Weick, K. E. (1993). The collapse of sensemaking in organizations: The Mann Gulch disaster. *Administrative Science Quarterly, 38,* 628-652.

Weick, K. E. (1995). Editing innovation into *Administrative Science Quarterly.* In L. L. Cummings & P. J. Frost (Eds.), *Publishing in the organizational sciences* (pp. 284-296). Thousand Oaks, CA: Sage.

Winsor, D. (1993). Constructing scientific knowledge in Gould and Lewontin's "The Spandrels of San Marco." In J. Selzer (Ed.), *Understanding scientific prose* (pp. 127-143). Madison: University of Wisconsin Press.

Wolcott, H. (1990). *Writing up qualitative research.* Newbury Park, CA: Sage.

Yan, A., & Gray, B. (1994). Bargaining power: Management control and performance in United States-China joint ventures—A comparative case study. *Academy of Management Journal, 37,* 1478-1717.

Index

About the Authors

Karen Golden-Biddle, Ph.D., is on the faculty of the Goizueta Business School at Emory University. She earned her Ph.D. in management and policy studies at Case Western Reserve University. Her research interests center on (a) how culture and identity shape organizational life and (b) the role of language in the construction of scientific knowledge, an area in which she has worked collaboratively with Karen Locke. She has published her work in journals such as *Organization Science, Journal of Management Studies, Human Resource Management, Nonprofit Management and Leadership,* and *Academy of Management Journal.* In her institutional roles, she is co-editor of the nontraditional research section of the *Journal of Management Inquiry,* is on the editorial board of the *Academy* *of Management Journal,* and serves as delegate-at-large for the research methods division of the Academy of Management.

Karen D. Locke, Ph.D., is Associate Professor of business administration at the College of William and Mary's business school. She joined the faculty there in 1989 after earning her Ph.D. in organizational behavior from Case Western Reserve University. She uses qualitative methods to pursue her research interests. Her investigative work focuses on the written construction of scientific work in the organizational studies community and on the examination of emotionality in the workplace. Working in partnership with Karen Golden-Biddle, she has explored how qualitative researchers achieve "convincing" manuscripts and how they textually create opportunities for unique contributions. Subsequent work will explore differences between qualitative and quantitative texts in the organization sciences. Her work on emotionality has examined how comedy transforms feelings in service provider/client relationships and transforms the feeling of doing emotionally difficult work. Her work has appeared in journals such as *Organization Science, Journal of Management Inquiry, Studies in Organization, Culture and Society,* and *Academy of Management Journal.*